BELIEVERS

Paul Collins is one of Australia's most controversial and respected commentators on the Catholic church. A graduate of Harvard Divinity School and the Australian National University, he is a former priest and a historian and broadcaster. Dr Collins is also a former specialist editor of religion for the Australian Broadcasting Corporation. His publications include *Mixed Blessings*, *No Set Agenda*, *God's Earth*, *Between the Rock and a Hard Place* and *Burn*.

*Dedicated to the young Catholics
of today, especially Tim, Zachary,
Nicholas, Lucinda Mary, Tom,
Jack and Will. Trusting that they
will inherit the riches of faith that
sustained us, and draw on it in their
own lives. And for Marilyn.*

PAUL COLLINS

BELIEVERS

Does Australian Catholicism have a future?

UNSW PRESS

A UNSW Press book
Published by
University of New South Wales Press Ltd
University of New South Wales
Sydney NSW 2052
AUSTRALIA
www.unswpress.com.au

National Library of Australia
Cataloguing-in-Publication entry
Collins, Paul, 1940– .
   Believers: does Australian Catholicism have a future.

   Bibliography.
   Includes index.
   ISBN 978 086840 831 6 (pbk.).

   1. Catholic Church - Australia. 2. Catholic Church -
   Australia - Controversial literature. 3. Catholics -
   Australia. I. Title.

282.94

Design Di Quick
Printer Griffin Press

This book is printed on paper using fibre supplied from plantation
or sustainably managed forests.

Contents

Foreword

Keep hope alive. It is probably Paul Collins' key message in *Believers*, his most constructive book yet. This is the work of a man on a mission, of a very modern sort. He issues a profound invitation to fellow Australian Catholics to gird our loins and seriously evaluate the role of faith in our lives. He makes the ultimate ask of us. He begs us for new energy, to believe the Church is worth our best renewed effort. He wants us to prioritise invigorating it, despite already over-full schedules. Instead of the foreboding that he says traps faithful Church people, inducing almost a depression about the future, he invites us to revisit our own tradition; to reassess the prospect of life in Australia *without* its influence. Catholicism in this country, he suggests, is unique in the English-speaking world in terms of reach into individual lives and impact on the needy parts of the community. Why is the extraordinary service that is offered to the community, Catholic and otherwise, not better acknowledged? I've never come up with a satisfactory answer. As an ideal model of the service and compassion offered by Jesus Christ, it so clearly trumps any accusation that the Australian arm of the institution has steadily, pathetically declined into an empty, self-serving vessel.

However, I'm no Pollyanna about this same Church. That's the trouble. Like Paul, it is embedded in my identity, which means I know all too well where it falls short. In my media life, I'm required to report on modern management developments, including the absolutely vital need to know and name your mission. In order to motivate those within as well as attract others, you must be able to refresh your troops with clearly articulated statements of purpose. It can be shallow but also forces a discipline and a sort of humility about re-examination. I see some effort on this score within the Church – with new diocesan plans and restructuring and so on. But really I see precious little genuine wrestling with how this institution could scale the heights, providing *meaning* to prosperous, contemporary Australia. This is surely its main mission. Having an option for the poor, which has governed Catholicism for generations, is still critical. But what about a *theology of plenty,* to meet the needs of laypeople doing well materially but who seek something more? Of course not everyone is sharing in the boom. But sufficient numbers of Catholics are, let's be honest, and they need a Church to meet them in their current dilemmas, not those that bedeviled their struggling parents. This requires courage. It is undeniably very hard work of the head and heart. Yes, it requires true faith. Here, Paul's emphasis on hope is so timely. He suggests we revisit the extraordinary beauty of the imagery offered by his biblical namesake, the great St Paul, who regarded hope as central: as the 'dynamism driving the whole of creation, the reality that brings us liberation when our bodies are set free from the anxiety that ripples through us and turns us into cynics'.

Will this bold challenge re-energise weary but faithful Catholics of, say, the Vatican II era, such as myself? Do we have the essential faith, Paul Collins seems to be asking, to bother? Many of us believe we've already travelled long and arduous journeys, intertwined with the Church's own, for the last four or so decades. Indeed we may have decided our personal faith development is a better bet than recommitting passionately, recklessly, to the institution itself. As one Canadian churchman put it recently in *The Tablet* (8 December 2007) those who don't recognise the Church as a source of hope will instead perceive it as a burden – one more burden they don't need in their overburdened lives.

This emphasis on durable hope means that in vital areas, he and Pope Benedict are very much on the same page, identifying the key ingredients for Catholicism to survive and thrive. In his December encyclical *Spe Salvi* ('Saving Hope'), the Pope chose to highlight hope as the critical virtue of

Christian life. More, he suggested it distinguished Christian existence from others. The one who has hope lives differently, he said. Could there be a more compelling summary of why Christian life matters to the modern world? Of course, the Pope did not suggest the Church was on the cusp of any real tipping-point of survival versus extinction, even though he regards re-evangelising Europe as his top priority. Paul Collins, however, is less coy about the serious challenges facing the Catholic Church in Australia. Without being apocalyptic, he lays out the evidence in terms of declining full-time personnel to celebrate the routine ballast of the Church: its irreplaceable ritual life. Additionally, the aging of priests, the lack of new candidates, the resistance to drawing back married, ordained men, the sheer size of Australian dioceses – all these devastating facts amount to a perfect storm on the pretty-close horizon. Yet inducing hopelessness is not his aim, though he does imply that it's about ten minutes to midnight.

He concludes there is a window of probably twenty years or so in which the Church can be reinvigorated as a vital backdrop to contemporary Australian life. He reminds us that churches in other regions throughout history, for example North Africa, have simply dwindled into irrelevance. It *could* happen here as the century unfolds. So if the Church is to remain a precious jewel in everyday life, passionate hope is the prerequisite – easier said than done.

It is less hard to imagine when one sees the Church community on display at its best. It has been my joy to behold this in my own parish context within the last year. During this time, my Sydney parish has welcomed a new priest of twelve months' standing, the ordination of another and the installation of our parish priest as a bishop. It has made for an unrepeatable (probably) opportunity for my fellow-parishioners, including my fourteen-year-old son, to sense the richness and plenitude of a Church-alive. The two liturgical services, especially the installation, were unforgettable: a pastorally orientated priest, rapturously welcomed at the door of St Mary's Cathedral, amid spontaneous, unscheduled clapping from hundreds of parishioners, their joy rolling up the pews to the altar to meet the startled but happy Cardinal George Pell, the main celebrant. If I'm not mistaken, the look on his face said it all: if only it was all like this! A much-loved shepherd enchanting his flock and wel-comed accordingly. You wish, I thought to myself at the time. Yet I do wish there were more chances to prompt my son's subsequent comments. Raising his head one night from *The Simpsons* (that other notable pulpit that offers many behavioural codes and moral fables), he proclaimed that the Catholic Church was clearly richer than all the others because of its unity. The Protes-tant churches seemed small and divided by contrast, he said. Ah yes, I replied, trying to sound wisely even-handed, but after all they did stress one-to-one relationships well in their individual parishes and notably looked after each other. No, it didn't persuade him. Size *did* matter in his eyes.

Of course it was a clerical Church on display during these big events, which always leaves me with seriously mixed feelings. If I'm honest, despite some satisfying sermons, I am increasingly moved by offerings from other *lay-people* rather than the clergy. They simply speak to my own daily dilemmas better, which is hardly surprising. And they are more full of hope than almost anyone inside the institutional Church. Also I see faith lived out more viv-idly in the Catholic schools I know than elsewhere in the Church. Never for-getting their Order histories, these are splendid lay venues, with incredibly imaginative, courageous, original versions of Catholicism on show, as Paul points out.

If we laypeople take our Vatican II theology seriously, we will step up to the plate more. We will answer the call, as Paul has outlined it, because we know well the parlous state of the institution, notwithstanding its ability to bounce back. Maybe *we're* the bounce this time round? Is there no other white knight? Could that be the awful conclusion Paul is begging us to draw? I've often wondered whether we laypeople do see ourselves as the core of the pil-grim Church, or not. So when some try hard to reinstate a more hierarchical Church, do we quietly retreat? Do we wonder if the game is worth the candle, that question of burden once more rearing its head, threatening our fragile cup of available energy?

Maybe it would help if we heard more serious reflection by Church officials about the nature of service, similar to that sparked by its then head in Australia, Fr Mark Raper S.J. About four years ago, at a seminar run by Monte Sant' Angelo school in North Sydney, conducted by the Mercy Nuns who educated me, Fr Raper developed an admirable thesis about the vocation of true clerical service to laypeople, not the other way round. The Jesuits, he said, had always tried to stand between the hierarchy and laypeople, as their particular mission inside the Church. Throughout their history, they had tried to discern where need in the Catholic community might have shifted, requiring a concomitant shift of focus from the Order. Their recent diagnosis of the Australian flock? That it needed increasing service, of a dedicated and subtly different sort, whose outlines were only now being developed. Fr Raper was clearly humbled by the implications of this vision. I don't blame him. It is demanding in the extreme: facilitating others' wellbeing and faith, harnessing personal ego, offering genuine compassion and duty without assured affirmation or glory. For the ambitious Jesuits, it represents a big step towards a new model of Church. It certainly gained my respect.

In all the copious debates about religion and society, one of the key questions is never properly canvassed: what would Australia feel like *without* an active, vaguely relevant Catholic Church? Correctly, there's interest in some of its poor legacies like sexual abuse. But consider the vacuum caused by the surrender of a hopeful Church, together with its ritual life, its routine generosity, its largeness of spirit, its roadmap for a *soul's* journey through life as opposed to Economic or Intellectual Man or Woman's Progress? Imagine the profound gap that would leave. Paul Collins' central challenge is not to broader society but to Catholics. Does any of this still matter seriously to us? See how these Christians *love* each other, was the Romans' awestruck observation of the earliest Church people. Maybe our version should be about hope. See how these 21st-century Catholics *hope* and how it revives them. And then how it encourages them to act as though there is more to life than meets the eye. This is the call that many of us can hardly bear to hear. We can but live in hope that some of us do.

Geraldine Doogue

Acknowledgments

Many people have helped in the writing of this, but I would especially like to acknowledge Bishop Patrick Power, Dr Anne O'Brien, Geraldine Doogue, Presentation Sister Michele Kennan, Amanda McKenna and Brian Coyne, Frank Purcell, Paul Flint, Kevin Walcot, Peter McArdle, Fathers Eric Hodgens, Frank Martin, John Ryan, Emmanuel Bonello, Peter Williams, Hal Ranger, Ian McGinty, and Sacred Heart Fathers John Leary and Bill Brady, as well as Bob Dixon and Audra Kunciunas of the Pastoral Projects Office, Sally Heath and Christine Moore of the National Council of Priests, Francis Sullivan and Catholic Health Australia, and the staff at MacKillop Catholic College, especially Rita Daniels (principal), Michele Marks, Paul Goonan and Mark Pickham and the community at Saint Thomas More's parish, Hadfield.

Acronyms

ABS	Australian Bureau of Statistics
ACBC	Australian Catholic Bishops' Conference
ACLRI	Australian Conference of Leaders of Religious Institutes
ALP	Australian Labor Party
AMA	Australian Medical Association
CACW	Council for Australian Catholic Women
CARA	Center for Applied Research in the Apostolate (Georgetown University)
CDF	Congregation for the Doctrine of the Faith
CEO	Catholic Education Office (diocesan)
DLP	Democratic Labor Party
NCEC	National Catholic Education Commission
NCP	National Council of Priests
OCW	Ordination of Catholic Women
PA	Pastoral Associate
RCIA	Rite of Christian Initiation of Adults
RE	Religious Education
SWAP	Sunday Worship in Absence of a Priest
USCCB	United States Conference of Catholic Bishops
Vatican II	Second Vatican Council (1962–65)
WYD08	World Youth Day 2008
YOTS	Youth Off the Streets

Introduction

Between 14 and 20 July 2008 Sydney will host an event that is predicted to attract larger crowds than the 2000 Olympic Games. But it's not a sporting event; it's a spiritual one sponsored by the Australian Catholic church. It's called World Youth Day 2008 (WYD08), even though it actually lasts for *six* days! More than half a million young people are expected to attend, many from interstate and overseas. When WYD was held in Cologne in mid-2006 in excess of 800 000 young people were there. Similar-sized crowds attended in Toronto in 2004. But it was the 1995 WYD in Manila that set the record with an attendance at the papal Mass of around 5 million people, probably the largest crowd in human history. In Rome in 2000 2.5 million people attended. The target group is those aged between 16 and 30, the generation most disaffiliated from the church.

Among those who are expected in Sydney is Pope Benedict XVI, a man who certainly lacks the drawing power and super-star status of Pope John Paul II, but who has nevertheless proved he can create a frisson with crowds, and he has the added status of the papal office. A large-scale preparation has been underway across Australia for 20 months involving young people, not all of them Catholic. The logistical problems have been enormous. The purpose of WYD is to educate and energise young people to go out into the world to witness to the Christian gospel. While not quite Billy Graham-style revivalism, there is a similar 'feel' to the event. Catholicism will be in the news, especially with the Pope in Sydney.

Clearly the Australian and New South Wales' governments think WYD08 is important: in April 2006 the federal government gave $20 million to the Sydney archdiocese to set up and run the WYD08 secretariat, and announced that it would waiver visa fees for international visitors attending. In August 2007 it gave an additional $15 million. The federal government will also bear the costs of security. The New South Wales government also passed an Act to set up a WYD Coordination Authority 'to provide for the co-operation of other government agencies in the planning, co-ordination and delivery of government services in relation to World Youth Day 2008 and related events'. Speaking to the Bill parliamentary secretary, Paul McLeay said, 'It is anticipated that around 500 000 people will participate ... including an expected 100 000 from overseas ... [It will be] bigger than the Rugby World Cup in terms of expected numbers. It is bigger than the Olympics, and it will take a similar level of co-ordination and services to make it happen.'[1] The event is expected to generate between $100 and $125 million for New South Wales' economy. The Bill easily passed the state Parliament with the only dissent in the Legislative Council from Democrat Arthur Chesterfield-Evans and Greens' Lee Rhiannon. Chesterfield-Evans argued that this was an explicitly Catholic event and that he was 'very keen on the separation of church and state' and that 'there should be no public moneys for the purpose of worship, teaching or observance of religious beliefs'. Rhiannon argued that Muslims would not be afforded the same public help if they staged something similar, and that it lacked any 'across-faith event' involving 'young people of all faiths and atheists'.[2] Presumably she means the event is insufficiently ecumenical. The only other significant protest came from the trainers (many of them Catholics) at Randwick Racecourse, the proposed site of the WYD papal Mass.

In fact Chesterfield-Evans and Rhiannon need not worry, for there is a sense in which the long-term spiritual effects of WYD are limited. It certainly provides young people with a chance to identify with Catholicism, and gives them a sense of belonging and pride through participation with their friends in a massive live event. Richard Rymarz, formerly of Australian Catholic University, who has studied the impacts of WYD likens those who travel long distances overseas to attend WYD to people on a pilgrimage. Central to the event will be the presence of the Pope. This will place Catholicism squarely, at least for a time, on the national agenda and in the media. But what long-term impact does the experience have on participants?

In one of the only studies available of the results of attendance at WYDs, Rymarz has followed-up the 4500 Australian pilgrims under the age of 18 who attended the Cologne event in 2005.[3] He makes a number of interesting points. Firstly, the young people who went to all the trouble and expense of going to Germany tended to come from committed and practising Catholic families. These young people

> had a higher incidence of a range of religious background behaviours such as Mass attendance, frequency of confession and membership of faith-based youth groups. Their responses to questions about the existence of God, inner life and spirituality … were all significantly different from those of the control group. It was suggested that these differences may largely be accounted for by the way in which pilgrims were selected.

Rymarz found that those who attended had a very positive response to the Cologne WYD and he suggests that this might have 'some similarity to the experience that many students have of secondary school retreats'. This involves being with a large group of friends, going to an interesting overseas venue and being engaged in challenging activities. Rymarz found that those who went to Cologne reported more involvement in their parishes and faith-based school activities after they returned. He sums it up by saying that they moved 'from an active to a committed model of affiliation'.

One young woman who attended WYD 2000 in Rome was Jo Grainger who gave up an intensive care nursing job after she returned to Australia to work full-time for the church. She told Radio National's *Encounter* program that

> The thing about youth in post-modern culture is that there are so many choices, there are so many options on a very grand scale and what I think John Paul II did very well was that he identified that young people want

something on this big grand scale – they like the grandness, they like the audio visual, they like the stimulation, the music, the culture. The youth numbers that are participating in Mass and things like that in our country are small. But when they go on World Youth Day they see a concept of the universal church – they see the fact that they are part of this massive huge thing called the universal church, the Catholic church, and I think that is what has the huge impact; so it is not a strategy, it is actually getting them in touch with more than just what they see at home … It is to know that what they see home is part of this big thing, this big picture.[4]

Work is now underway to establish a baseline for measuring the impact of WYD in Sydney when the number of young Australians involved will be far in excess of the active Catholic group that went to Cologne. This will be the real test. My own guess is that just like papal visits in the past, it will be a very positive experience for most participants. As Rymarz says, it will be like a school retreat. Perhaps for a tiny minority it will be a life-changing event, but most will revert to their previous patterns of existence before WYD with a lingering positive memory of living Catholicism.

However, WYD will do little to confront the real issues facing the Australian church, nor will it bring about the kinds of change needed to push local Catholicism in the direction of renewal. Fundamental change doesn't occur through spectacular events, but only through deep reflection, careful planning and a willingness to tackle deep-seated problems. That is what *Believers* aims to do. Using the opportunity of WYD, it sets out to reflect on Catholicism in Australian life and asks hard questions about the future of the church on our continent. For my entire life I have participated actively in Catholicism, and since the early 1980s I've written and talked publicly about the Australian and world church. What I aim to do in this book is to ask some of the questions from an independent, but well-informed, insider's perspective that official church people find hard to ask and confront, and the young are too inexperienced to know or articulate.

Personally, I must admit that as I look back over a lifetime dedicated to Catholicism, I feel a certain sense of disappointment. This is especially true as I reflect on the last two decades. So many opportunities and so much time has been lost. I am particularly sad for the enormous number of people who have given up on the church, who were once so enthusiastic and expended so much energy in their parishes, schools and Catholic organisations. These are the people from the pre- and post-World War II generations born between 1930 and 1960. These are the classic 'Vatican II Catholics', the people who lived through the greatest revolution in Catholic life since the 16th-century Reformation. Many of them are still my friends, but they are no longer involved in the life of the church. It's not that they don't feel a real sense of loss. Catholicism was part of the fabric of their being. But they consider that by staying they are compromised by the contemporary church. Of course there are some who have simply drifted away, but most have made conscious and painful decisions to leave the practise of Catholicism behind, even if they still think of themselves as 'cultural Catholics'. It's not something you jettison easily.

Having said that, the Catholic church can be an extraordinarily frustrating institution. Many of its problems are completely self-inflicted. For instance, while there is overwhelming evidence in Australia and elsewhere of a desperate shortage of priestly pastoral leadership in parishes and other ministries, a shortage that in Latin America is leading to the defection of literally millions of Catholics to fundamentalist Protestantism, church authorities still hang onto the requirement of celibacy as a precondition for ordination. This requirement was imposed on the clergy of the western church in the 11th century for reasons that make absolutely no sense today. Even then it had nothing to do with improving the spiritual or moral life of priests. Celibacy was used in the 11th century as a way of maintaining a primitive form of ritual purity, and of preventing the alienation of church property by laity and stopping priest-fathers from passing on their parishes to their priest-sons.[5] Nowadays the requirement of celibacy is seen for what it is: a requirement of church law that could be changed today. But despite the massive shortage of priests and the fact that a large majority of the Australian bishops would ordain properly trained married men immediately, they are hamstrung by popes and Roman authorities who stolidly refuse to face up to the problem of the shortage of clergy.

In the process Catholicism is in danger of losing aspects of its essential core: that is, worship, Mass and the Sacraments, the very heart of the church, and a defining element of what it means to be Catholic. Yet in order to hang onto celibacy senior ecclesiastics refuse to train and ordain suitable married men to lead that worship. And they do this in face of the fact that the vast majority of Jesus' apostles and disciples were married, including the first pope, Saint Peter, as were by far the greater number of priests and bishops in the first 1100 years of the church's existence. So while it is clear to the vast majority of sensible Catholics that the church must change its policy on celibacy, church authorities still resist the patently obvious. Why?

Experienced church lawyer and former Sydney Auxiliary Bishop Geoffrey Robinson stated that

> I believe that the Catholic church is in a prison … It constructed the prison for itself, locked itself in and threw away the key. That prison is the prison of not being able to be wrong … Far too often the Catholic church believed that it had such a level of divine guidance that it did not need the right to be wrong … even when clear evidence emerges that earlier decisions were conditioned by their own time and that the arguments for them are not as strong as they were once thought to be.[6]

Robinson was speaking within the context of sexual abuse, but his comments have a wider resonance. This imprisonment in the past has been reinforced by the doctrine of infallibility, which also conveys a sense that the church can never be wrong. It is precisely this that the church needs to confront. Yet, at the same time, historically Catholicism has shown a great ability to survive crises of all sorts, including its self-inflicted problems and stupidity. The paradox is that while tearing our hair out in frustration, many of us have stayed, simply because we feel at home in a church that is such a failed, scarred and sinful institution. This is why I have always found church history so helpful: not only does it show the church's high points, but also reveals the depths to which it has sunk and still survived.

In a way this book is the most recent in a series of reflections on Australian and worldwide Catholicism. Having written so much about the need for change in the church, I must admit I am sometimes tempted by pessimism. As this book makes clear I believe that we are at a turning point, a crisis of decision in the life of the Australian church. It is not as though well-informed Catholics have not been aware of all of these issues for many years. Perhaps my own disappointment can be traced back to the fact that in my books *Mixed Blessings* (1986) and *No Set Agenda* (1991) I highlighted the issues of alienation of Catholics and crisis in the church years ago. *Mixed Blessings* was published in 1986 in preparation for the visit of Pope John Paul II to Australia later that year. It told the story of the Second Vatican Council (1962–65) and of all that happened in the years since the Council concluded. It also looked to the future and discussed the trajectory that the papacy of John Paul II (1978–2005) might take. The tragedy is that, whatever its successes, the 27-year-long Wojtyla papacy actually developed into a kind of holding pattern; virtually nothing was done to confront the serious internal issues facing Catholicism (such as the priest shortage). In fact, there was a real retreat from what had already been achieved since the close of Vatican II. In *No Set Agenda* I pointed out that

> there are many signs that the Australian church has entered a perilous
> period in its development. Catholicism is not facing an external crisis, but
> a loss of confidence and self-identity. The core of the problem is that the
> Catholic church has become lethargic and passionless; it has lost its sense
> of direction … It has turned in on itself.[7]

I was still optimistic then that the church might recover, and that serious change was a possibility. I argued that Catholicism in the early 1990s had entered a decisive period when hard choices would have to be made for survival and when far-reaching decisions about the church's trajectory in Australian society had to be taken. But clearly nobody with any real influence was listening.

We are now a decade-and-a-half further down the track. While there is no doubt that the universal church will survive – in many places Catholicism is prospering – that does not mean that every local church will make it. In the past large regional churches have disappeared. An example is the decimation of Christian North Africa after the Muslim invasions in the 7th century. The reason for the massive losses is that between the 4th and 6th centuries the church in the region had become immersed in theological obsessions and disputes that bore little or no relationship to spirituality and the essence of living the faith. Eastern Christianity was irreparably divided and profoundly vulnerable to Islam. And almost the whole of North Africa was lost. So while I believe that the future of universal Catholicism is assured, this is not necessarily true of every local branch, including the Australian one. The danger is that while ecclesiastical structures would survive, the church here could become a mere shell and shadow of its former self. Or it might withdraw into a sectarian rump peopled by the so-called 'orthodox'.

In contrast, it could also renew itself and draw on the incredible ability of Catholicism not only to survive, but to find in the very process of dying, renewed life. As Jesus tells Martha before raising Lazarus from the dead 'Those who believe in me, even though they die, will live, and everyone who lives and believes in me will never die' (John 11:25–26). In my optimistic moments I have the feeling that we might just be at one of those dying and living moments when the situation is fluid enough for real change to occur. Ultimately I'm optimistic that it is not too late, and that we have to seize the opportunity that the crisis of decision gives us. As *Believers* shows, Australian Catholicism has both strengths and weaknesses as it faces its decision and its destiny. The book was written as a contribution to debate about the future.

1

Catholicism in action

This may seem a strange place to begin a reflection on Catholicism in action, but homeless people often have terrible problems with their feet. This is because they have to walk everywhere, often carrying heavy loads, and because they cannot afford proper footwear they regularly use ill-fitting shoes, boots, or sandals. Twenty podiatrists volunteer to care for the homeless men who seek shelter or come for free meals at Matthew Talbot Hostel in a lane off Corfu Street in Woolloomooloo in inner Sydney. This is not the most salubrious part of the city, but is close to the CBD, the Domain and Botanic Gardens and every day men stand outside, some patient, some agitated, most smoking, waiting to see if they can get one of the 112 beds that Matthew Talbot has available. In 2005 the Hostel was refurbished and many now have private rooms. The Hostel, which began in 1938, also provides a free health clinic staffed by volunteer nurses and doctors, a service run for 30 years by Dr Ian Webster, professor of public health at the University of New South Wales. Webster says 'I get more pleasure talking to a homeless person than a business executive. There is no artificiality and no falsehoods.' Homeless people often have serious health needs and are more likely to suffer injuries on the street. Matthew Talbot has a laundry, as well as government and legal services. Every day it provides more than 700 free hot meals.

Matthew Talbot Hostel is run by a small, mainly part-time staff and over 380 members and volunteers from the Saint Vincent de Paul Society. The Society's own research shows that

Existing stereotypes of homelessness as an aging man with a dependence on alcohol are no longer relevant. The average age of a single homeless man today is just 35 years but single women both young and old, young single parent families and those escaping domestic violence are also in danger of finding themselves on the brink of homelessness or homeless.

Contributing factors are drought, rural poverty, mental health issues, depression, domestic violence, addiction, family and relationship breakdown and financial pressure. Many people are on the street because of the closure of public mental institutions. They suffer from moderate to severe psychiatric illnesses, often linked to drug or alcohol problems.

Matthew Talbot Hostel is just one of the works of the Saint Vincent de Paul Society. 'Vinnies' (as it is known in Australia) is a Catholic lay organisation, founded in Paris in 1833 by Frédéric Ozanam, a literary scholar, professor at the Sorbonne and a progressive Catholic, to support and care for the poor. It was introduced into Australia in 1854. The growth here has been remarkable. In 2007 there were 19 516 members and volunteers in New South Wales and the Australian Capital Territory, 7973 in Queensland, 7682 in Victoria and 7300 in the other states and the Northern Territory.[1] Nationwide there are almost 42 500 members and volunteers, easily making it Australia's largest charity. Members serve through local parish 'conferences' in which social and class distinctions are ignored. In the Conference meeting Vincentian spirituality and prayer is closely linked to work for those most in need. 'Need' is the only test applied. No one is asked about their religion, race, social status, gender preference, or belief. The local conference works through home visitation and directly assists needy families and people with food vouchers and the payment of bills. These parish-based conferences are free of clerical control; this is the work of self-directed laity whose aim is to live out their Christian call to service through meeting the needs of those most marginalised in society. Volunteers don't have to be Catholics; in some places more than half are not. They are usually associated with one specific work of the Society. Some of the Society's funding comes from government sources, but its ethos is rooted within Catholicism, and it still relies heavily on church and community for financial support.

What is extraordinary is the range of services offered by Vinnies in New South Wales and the Australian Capital Territory. Its 37 facilities provide 692 beds and 36 outreach programs: 14 facilities for single, homeless men (356 beds), six for single women (48 beds), five for families (49 beds and cots), two for men with children (22 beds and cots), seven for women with children (199 beds and cots), and two for young people (18 beds). On an average day 150 people are turned away from Vinnies' homeless services in New South Wales alone. In Sydney, Liverpool and other New South Wales towns night patrols provide sandwiches and warm drinks as well as friendship for people sleeping rough.[2]

In the other states and territories the Society provides parallel services. In Victoria Vinnies offers a wide range of assistance including aged care and disability services, home visitation, financial and food assistance, migrant and refugee support, homeless accommodation, soup vans that support about 450 homeless people every night, centres for youth and overseas projects. The Melbourne equivalent of Matthew Talbot is Ozanam House on Flemington Road, North Melbourne with 63 beds. As well as homeless services the Society also provides cheap clothing, furniture and other necessities through 619 centres or shop fronts across Australia, which are also used to raise money to support the Society's work. The total number of people annually assisted by Vinnies is an extraordinary 1.8 million.[3]

While the Society is primarily geared to service at the coalface, Vinnies' leadership has been increasingly willing to confront the structural issues that lead to poverty and deprivation in the first place. While this has caused considerable debate, nowadays the Society's leadership is willing to speak out. The Salvation Army provides similar services and they are very up-front about publicising their activities. In contrast, Vinnies are unobtrusive, publicity-shy, de-centralised, less hierarchical, and far less obviously prominent. They represent Catholicism at its best.

I have begun this book with homelessness and the Saint Vincent de Paul

Society because it is so easy to caricature Catholicism as a self-interested monolith divorced from the wider community and out of touch with the experiences of people. Many outsiders think the church is one entity controlled from Rome with the pope at its apex, the bishops as local managers and all its activities hierarchically controlled. This is where Vinnies provides a contrasting perspective. It is a genuinely lay-run organisation where clerical influence is almost non-existent. It is often forgotten that Catholicism is not a centralised corporation, but a complex interlocking constellation of different, semi-independent entities: lay organisations, religious orders, dioceses, parishes, schools, hospitals and other ministries, all with their own legal status, independent finances and administration. Certainly, since the mid-19th century Catholicism has become more over-centralised than ever before in its history; nevertheless many parts of the church are still independent. What holds the structure together is a common belief in the person of Jesus Christ, a sense of belonging to the community he founded, and of trying to live a life open to God through care for others. Catholicism also entails a commitment to the church and to its teaching and leadership. Catholics believe that it is Christ's spirit that holds the whole communion together.

Most of this, of course, is never articulated, even by Catholics themselves. Often the church is portrayed in the media as a self-engrossed institution without any recognition of what it has achieved and is achieving in Australian society. Part of the reason is the sheer diversity of the services that the church offers, which at times seem to have little connection with Catholicism. As a result, the media and the broader community tend to disassociate these services from institutional Catholicism. But it is the church and the Christian call to service that gives all of these their *raison d'etre*. So before we tackle some of the hard issues the church faces in Australia, I want to give some sense of Catholicism in action, and look at its wide range of services.

Saint Vincent de Paul is the largest Catholic charity. There are many others. For instance, in the heart of Melbourne's St Kilda, parts of which are a 'red light' district, Sacred Heart Mission provides 300 to 400 people with a three-course lunch every day. It all began in 1982 in the presbytery kitchen next to the Italian Renaissance-style church when Father Ernie Smith, then parish priest, started feeding lonely people from local boarding houses.[4] He told *The Age* (19/5/03) that many people 'had landed in rooming houses without any support. It was a world of loneliness I discovered. People used to say St Kilda was a bad place, but I'd say 'No, it's not a bad place, it's a sad place'.' Numbers for the meals grew and Smith and his helpers soon had to move into the parish hall. The meals not only offer nutrition, but also try to build community and create social connections among homeless people. The work is largely done by volunteers from all faiths (and none), with a small number of paid staff. Among them are people assigned by the courts to perform community service orders, some of whom return to continue the work after their sentences expire. Nowadays the Mission still provides food, clothing, emergency relief, accommodation, medical help, counselling, aged care, affordable housing, home visits, sport, recreation, and even an Australian rules team, 'The Hearts'. The women's program helps those working as prostitutes, as well as drug-addicted and abused women, through support and the provision of housing. It has now taken over the presbytery, and the priest lives elsewhere. In 2006 Sacred Heart Mission served 137 099 meals.

Father Chris Riley began his work for youth in Sydney. He founded and developed Youth Off the Streets (YOTS). A member of the Salesians of Don Bosco, an Italian-founded religious order devoted to the care of youth, Chris Riley worked for many years as a school teacher and then as principal of Boy's Town at Engadine in southern Sydney with difficult youngsters sent there by the courts. In 1991 he left Engadine for Kings Cross to begin working full-time on the streets with chronically homeless young people. YOTS grew out of this and has adopted innovative approaches to the abused and traumatised girls and boys with whom it deals through street-based programs and drug and alcohol rehabilitation in rural settings. After the tsunami in Aceh, despite enormous difficulties involved in working in a conservative Muslim region, Riley managed to set up the first shelter for children orphaned by the disaster.[5] While he is still the inspiration and CEO of YOTS, the organisation is non-sectarian and open to all-comers. Nevertheless it is the Christian vision as inspired by Saint John Bosco, founder of the Salesians, of service to the poorest children that inspires Riley and almost 150 staff and over 800 volunteers.

Australia already has one saint, Blessed Mary MacKillop. Many think the second should be a Wiradjuri woman from Cowra in central-western New South Wales, Colleen Shirley Smith, known to everyone as 'Mum Shirl'. Over the years Mum Shirl influenced Father Ted Kennedy at Saint Vincent's parish in Sydney's Redfern, when he turned the resources of the church over to caring for dispossessed urban Aborigines. Extremely well read in theology and literature, Ted Kennedy described Mum Shirl at her funeral in 1998 in Saint Mary's Basilica as 'The greatest theologian I have ever known.' She had taught Kennedy how to fight for justice. Mum Shirl didn't suffer fools gladly, and quickly brought the mighty and righteous down from their thrones, often with some well-placed four-letter words. Before joining Redfern parish, Mum Shirl had been a prison visitor for years and she had raised as her own more than 60 children who came into her care. She worked with the Redfern parish to establish the Aboriginal medical and legal services that now operate next-door to the church. The *Encyclopedia of Aboriginal Australia* says that her

> work at Saint Vincent's evolved into an informal welfare agency for a mixed
> clientele of ex-prisoners, children in need, single parents, alcoholics and
> young probationers. With no money of her own, she often ran her services
> on her own sickness benefits ... By the 1990s Mum Shirl had assisted some
> 6000 people.[6]

It is worth remembering this because the churches generally, and the Catholic church specifically, are often criticised for their mission work with Aborigines. It is true that the record is mixed and Catholics were often paternalistic and destructive of culture and language. Given the criticism the church often receives, it is worth reviewing briefly the historic relationship between Catholicism and Aborigines. Certainly in the 19th century the church attempted to convert as well as protect Aborigines. For instance John Bede Polding, Sydney's first archbishop, was deeply concerned about what was happening to

Aborigines, but he lacked the resources to do much about the situation. In 1863 he wrote to the Spanish Benedictine, Bishop Rosendo Salvado, one of the pioneer monks at New Norcia in Western Australia, about Aboriginal dispossession by white settlers:

> Alas! The march of European civilization is the march of desolation [for Aborigines], and unless means are used which our Liberals repudiate, the black savage will be exterminated to make place for a white savage – far more ruthless. They are shot down in Queensland like wild dogs – and with as little remorse. Even poison has been used.[7]

In his 1869 Pastoral Letter Polding bluntly told Catholics that

> We have dispossessed the Aboriginals of the soil. In natural justice, then, we are held to compensation … [the church desires] solemnly to lay upon the conscience of all who have property in these colonies the thought that there is blood upon their land, and that human souls to whom they are in so many ways debtors in the name of natural justice, and in the name of the Redeemer, are perishing because no man careth for them.[8]

Admittedly, Polding and other churchmen who genuinely cared about the Aborigines wanted to settle them on missions and convert them. But what is clear is that prelates like Polding were unwilling to allow white depredation and murder pass without condemnation.

Salvado had tried to learn local languages and was sympathetic to Aboriginal spirituality. He realised that Aborigines in Northern Australia were still remote from the corruption of European settlers and he and Polding wanted to get in first and establish missions there. In 1882, the Jesuits made an attempt to establish a base at Rapid Creek (now a Darwin suburb), moving to the Daly River in 1886. But recurrent floods forced them to withdraw in 1899.[9] It was not until the appointment of the French priest, Francis Xavier Gsell, as apostolic administrator in 1906 and as bishop of Darwin in 1938, that something permanent was achieved. An intelligent and patient man, Gsell worked hard to understand and appreciate Aboriginal habits, customs, rituals and spiritual values.[10] As a member of the religious order, the Missionaries of the Sacred Heart, Gsell brought his colleagues to the Northern Territory and the order staffed all territory missions and parishes until the last two decades. Unfortunately, Gsell's successor, Bishop John O'Loughlin, was influenced by government assimilationist policies and was opposed to missionaries learning Aboriginal languages.

One who worked his way around this was Father John Leary. He first went to Port Keats (Wadeye), in 1958 and spent a total of 15 years there in two stints.[11] Wadeye was founded in 1935 in a remote area on the Joseph Bonaparte Gulf, 400 kilometres south-west of Darwin. Leary began learning Murinbata, Port Keats' language, and spent much time in the bush with the local people. He came to admire their incredible bush skills and deep spirituality and realised that knowing the language was the only way to understand what they were thinking. The O'Loughlin prohibition didn't prevent Leary, as well as Father Mervyn Bailey, working on the Murinbata language.[12] While the assimilationist policy was destructive, Leary is equally critical of the policies begun under the Whitlam government in the 1970s. People were brought into the mission for education. The emphasis was on learning a European curriculum and it was essentially whites teaching Aborigines how to get on in modern Australian society. As a result, Aborigines gradually lost their self-confidence, and the younger people have become confused and lost. They lack traditional knowledge and bush skills, and are caught between the two cultures. While motivated by goodwill and sincerity, there was as much unconscious paternalism operative in this government policy as there was in past assimilationist policies. Modern education and government policy, as much as Catholicism, has contributed to the destruction of traditional culture.

The church took the same approach in Western Australia. Here the German-born Pallottine missionary, Father Ernest Ailred Worms, spent two long stints in the Kimberley region between 1930 and 1957. He was one of the great students of Aboriginal religion. His book, *Australian Aboriginal Religions*, remains a basic text to this day.[13] Professor WEH 'Bill' Stanner, the other great Australian expert on Aboriginal religion, sums up the missionary approach to Aboriginal belief. He says that some missionaries had no feel for Aboriginal religions; others were very sensitive to it. None, he says, 'could compare with, let alone exceed that of the late Father Worms'.[14]

It is also true that the churches played a role in the 'stolen generations' policy whereby Aboriginal children were taken from their parents by the state. But the participation of the churches must be seen within the perspective of broader social attitudes of white Australians towards Aborigines in the decades before the 1960s. At its most benign the general attitude was assimilation, at its worst it was elimination, either by neglect or even deliberate murder. Two of the most recent massacres were the Forest River massacre in early-June 1926 just west of Wyndham, Western Australia, and the Coniston massacres lasting through August–September 1928 on the edge of the Tanami Desert, north-west of Alice Springs. Both were carried out by European police assisted by graziers. The official figures are that 11 people were killed at Forest River and 17 at Coniston. Here the central figure was Mounted Constable William George Murray. Despite official figures there is no doubt that many more Aborigines were killed, up to 100 at Forest River and possibly up to 200 by Murray and his posse. He was exonerated and died in Adelaide in the 1980s.[15] These are the last massacres we know about, but there were probably others within living memory. It is within this context that at least the missions provided a place of physical safety for Aboriginal people. Certainly this is the view of TGH Strehlow who at the end of his life 'rejected the polemical view that the missions ... should be seen as the villains of colonial history' because, in Strehlow's own words, it was the missions 'who protected the black populations from the rifles of other white settlers and the police'.[16]

From the 1970s onwards, attitudes changed radically in the Catholic church. The turning point was Pope John Paul II's speech in Alice Springs on 29 November 1986. This address was remarkable in that it unequivocally recognised that Aboriginal people had lived for thousands of years 'in spiritual closeness to the land, with its animals, birds, fishes, water holes, rivers, hills and mountains'. Referring to the dreamtime and to the spiritual value of Aboriginal stories, the Pope said they were 'not unlike some of the great inspired lessons from the people among whom Jesus himself was born'. He even bought into the *terra nullius* dispute recalling that Archbishop Polding 'opposed the legal fiction adopted by European settlers' and pointed out that he had 'pleaded for the rights of the Aboriginal inhabitants to keep the traditional lands on which their whole society depended'. The Pope confronted the assimilationist polices of the past and reached out to the stolen generations: 'Aboriginal people were transported from their homelands into small areas or reserves where families were broken up, tribes split apart, children orphaned and people forced to live like exiles in a foreign country.' He referred to the problems urbanised Aborigines faced that resulted from these displacement policies. He stressed that the gospel of Jesus embraced all cultures and encouraged his listeners to be 'through and through' Aboriginal Christians while still being 'faithful to your worthy traditions'. There is no doubt that this speech was written in Australia and that it represents the church's official view. It would have also been approved by the Vatican. The Pope placed the Catholic church squarely on the side of the Aborigines, and since that day in Alice Springs there has been no going back on this issue for Australian Catholics.

There are a surprising number of Aboriginal and Torres Strait Islander Catholics in Australia. Based on the 2001 census there are 94 800. This is 23.1 per cent of the Aboriginal population of Australia. This is a considerable increase from 1986 when 20.4 per cent of Aborigines identified as Catholics, but this is probably due to improved data collection rather than a rash of conversions. In the 2007 census there were about 105 000 Aboriginal and Torres Strait Islander Catholics in Australia. In 2001 the largest populations of Aboriginal Catholics were in New South Wales (33 422), followed by Queensland (22 428), Western Australia (17 305) and the Northern Territory (10 733).[17] Nowadays virtually every diocese has a dedicated Aboriginal ministry. This ministry is well-organised nationally.

One of the tragedies of Catholicism's recent work with Aborigines is the conflict that has developed at Saint Vincent's Redfern since the death of Father Ted Kennedy. This has been caused by the introduction of the Neo-

Catechumenate movement into the parish by the archdiocese of Sydney. Founded in Spain in 1964 as a lay movement, the 'Neo-Cats', as they're popularly known, believe that 'ordinary' Catholics are insufficiently 'committed' and need many more years of formation. In many parishes the Neo-Cats have a history of divisiveness and sectarianism. Also, many of the Neo-Cats are from overseas and this appears to have led them to not fully appreciating the process that Australian Catholics have been through, especially in regard to the relationship with Aboriginal people. The result is that in Redfern they seem to lack cultural sensitivity to the local Aborigines, and, for that matter, to the whites who have made the parish their home. But the ultimate responsibility for this tragic situation lies with the archdiocese and its determination to impose the Neo-Cats on the parish.

Nowadays when spirituality is mentioned, most Australians think of Buddhism with its traditions of meditation. Buddhist monks and nuns in their colourful robes are easily identified in the street and media. Many identify Christianity with a moralistic, dogmatic, evangelistic approach to faith. The long tradition of Catholic spirituality, which is culturally compatible with the Western tradition, is largely unknown even within the church itself.

One of the positive signs in contemporary society is the interest in meditation and spirituality. Some of the most widely read and well-known spiritual writers today are Catholics such as the American monk Thomas Merton, the English Benedictine, Bede Griffiths, who lived on a Christian *ashram* or hermitage in India, and Thomas Moore the American author of the best-selling book, *Care of the Soul* (1992). What we have seen in Catholicism in the last half century is a democratising of spirituality. This is a profoundly significant change for previously spirituality was what nuns, brothers and priests did and was seen as typical of religious orders, especially contemplative orders, rather than of the laity. There have been other periods in history when lay spirituality was prominent, and this is especially characteristic of our time.

As part of the contemporary revival, religious orders, dioceses and lay communities operate prayer and retreat houses across Australia. The webpage *A Quiet Place* lists 75, and there are a number not listed including some that are more ecumenically-oriented.[18] Typical of Catholic retreat and spirituality centres is Saint Mary's Towers, Douglas Park, New South Wales, which is run by the Missionaries of the Sacred Heart. It is 70 kilometres south of central Sydney right on the Hume Freeway. Between 800 and 1000 people per year attend various programs at Douglas Park including prayer weekends, six- and eight-day retreats and month-long silent programs including the Spiritual Exercises of Saint Ignatius Loyola and the Life's Journey Experience. The emphasis is very much on silence and contemplation and many of the participants are laypeople. A woman theology graduate who visits Douglas Park regularly, says that she goes because there is good liturgy, helpful, non-directive spiritual guidance from a laywoman who understands her situation, a respect for silence and 'five hundred hectares of solitude'. One of the priests there, Father Chris Chaplin, says that the people who come are thirsting to encounter God and to experience contemplative prayer. There is a sense in which they have moved beyond the church and, as Pope Saint Gregory the Great (590–604) says, are consumed with a passionate desire for the divine. Many feel that the institutional church has lost the sense of searching for God.

Further south near Bungendore, New South Wales is the Silver Wattle House of Prayer which has been run by a community of laypeople since 1976 for the archdiocese of Canberra–Goulburn. It offers people from all faiths or none a chance to spend time in prayer and reflection, and a chance to experience living in a Christian community. Mary MacKillop's Australian-founded Sisters of Saint Joseph (the 'Brown Joeys') have 11 spirituality and retreat centres across Australia, and the Jesuits have five focusing on the spirituality developed by their founder, Saint Ignatius Loyola. Many other religious orders have similar centres devoted to their spiritual tradition. While there is great interest in methods of prayer, meditation and the teaching of great mystics such as Saints Francis of Assisi, John of the Cross, Teresa, Ignatius Loyola and Dame Julian of Norwich, the emphasis in Catholic spirituality is shifting nowadays toward an awareness of the natural world and of God's special presence in creation. The profound sense of presence that we intuit in Australian landscape increasingly informs the kind of sensibility that characterises modern spirituality.

The interest shown in the film *Into Great Silence* about the Carthusian monks of the Grand Chartreuse south-east of Grenoble, indicates a kind of hunger for the absolute that is not being fulfilled by post-modern culture.

> The film has been a huge hit, not only in New York but also in allegedly secular Europe ... There is a spiritual hunger that goes deep. Some of its expressions can be shallow, but the need is heartfelt and real. Many churches may not meet it, but some places and ways of life (monasteries and monasticism, for example) attract people because they offer the hope that there is an answer to an eternal, deeply felt need.[19]

Interest in the contemplative aspects of life is a new development among Australians. In the past it was activism that was valued by Catholics. As a result we only have one truly contemplative order of priests: the Trappists at Tarrawarra near Yarra Glen, east of Melbourne. Among religious women there are at least six contemplative groups, the largest being the Discalced Carmelite Nuns with 10 convents spread across all the states, and the Benedictine Nuns at Jamberoo, New South Wales, who recently featured in *The Abbey* on ABC television, when five ordinary Australian women join the sisters of an enclosed, contemplative order for 33 days.

There are also a number of Australians living as hermits in the Catholic tradition. These are not just mad isolationists who have turned their back on the world, but people who have gone into the wilderness seeking a deeper encounter with God and themselves through a disciplined, solitary life. There are always people around to whom this kind of contemplative experience appeals, but few are able to fulfill their ambition. This may be because of family or personal commitments, or an inability to discern if this is what God is calling them to. Few reach the point of being able to say 'yes'. One member of a religious order who had lived a hermit's life for several years told me that the practicalities can be overcome and that God will pull it all together if the person ultimately makes the commitment. Inevitably most of those who do embrace the hermit's life are usually members of active religious orders who have training in self-discipline and a background in community. Really, you can only live alone after you have lived peacefully and joyously with others. Hermits live in all types of places, from the back of a church, to a hut at the back of a convent, to small houses in isolated areas.

One aspect of the work of religious orders that is often overlooked is the social justice work of religious women and men. Most religious orders have an aging membership, but that has not stopped them being very active outside institutional Catholicism. For instance the Brown Josephite Sisters were among the first to take up the cause of the East Timorese under Indonesian occupation when this was not a popular cause, and long before official Australian intervention. Quite a number of women's religious orders have been active in the area of stopping international trafficking of women and children for prostitution, especially focused on Australia. Again they were involved long before this issue became a matter of public knowledge due to the film *The Jammed*. Orders have also been active in the area of spirituality and the environment. The Christian Brothers have been especially active here.

But the spheres where the church has been most involved are health care, parishes and education. Firstly, health care. Catholicism plays a major role in the provision of health services in Australia, running the largest non-government health and aged care network in the country.[20] Most of this is funded by government. In January 2007, this led to a minor contretemps following an article in *The Australian* by the then Australian Medical Association (AMA) federal president, Mukesh Haikerwal, who criticised Catholic public hospitals because they did not provide a full range of medical services. Haikerwal claimed he had referred a patient to Mercy Hospital in the Melbourne suburb of Werribee for a kidney stone treatment, but the patient also wanted a vasectomy which the Catholic-run hospital was unwilling to carry out. The man had to travel 40 kilometres to Geelong for the vasectomy. Haikerwal's criticism was that Catholic public hospitals that don't offer the full range of medical services because these are not permitted by the church, should not be publicly funded. He was supported by Senators Lyn Allison (Democrat) and

Kate Lundy (Australian Labor Party) who argued that if Catholic hospitals are publicly funded they should align their ethics to those of the public sector. This is not new territory for Allison. Earlier she had argued that

> Religious service provision can mean some clients are denied services available elsewhere. In Bendigo, the now Catholic church run public hospital, will not do vasectomies, tubal ligations, or abortions, though they are legal and routine in other public hospitals ... This is discrimination.[21]

In response Francis Sullivan of Catholic Health Australia pointed out that Haikerwal, Allison and Lundy had ignited 'another "anti-Catholic" bashing exercise' and accused them of painting an untrue picture 'of a harsh and insensitive service devoid of compassion and decency'.[22] Sullivan argued that there are 'longstanding agreements' with governments of both persuasions that are 'respectful of the ethical position of the Catholic church'. He pointed out that not all public hospitals provide every form of service, and that the AMA itself insists that 'publicly funded GPs not be forced to prescribe the morning-after pill or give referrals to abortion clinics. They readily support the ethical independence of doctors – why take cheap shots at Catholic hospitals?' He argued that 'Unlike other private operators, the Catholic church conducts hospitals to meet community need, not shareholder greed' and that its 74 hospitals 'are spread over urban and regional Australia' and 'are enmeshed in local communities'. It was a storm in a teacup, but it focused the concerns that secularists like Allison and Lundy have about the work of Catholicism in Australian society.

The Catholic approach is not-for-profit and one of its foundational principles explicitly emphasises that 'Heath care is not a mere commodity open to entrepreneurial manipulation or the result of commercial profit making.' Its vision is that Christ's 'healing ministry flourishes as an integral part of the mission of the Catholic church'. It is community-oriented, is based on social justice and respect for the dignity of the human person and follows Catholic social teaching in its 'preferential option for the poor'. In other words there is 'a concern for the provision of adequate, timely health care for all, especially those who have little choice, opportunity or capacity to pay'. Many of the hospitals and health services were originally run independently by religious orders of women, such as the Sisters of Charity who established the first organised Catholic social welfare in Australia in 1839 when they began visiting the convict Female Factory in Parramatta. Nowadays most of these orders have formed various types of professional structures, but they usually work in co-operation through Catholic Health Australia, an umbrella organisation that liaises with the Australian Catholic Bishops' Conference (ACBC).

The Catholic hospital sector includes 73 heath care facilities with just over 9000 beds. This is made up of 21 public hospitals which are largely funded by state governments and cater for free public patients. There are also 52 privately funded hospitals in which about 80 per cent of patients pay for treatment through their medical insurance and about 20 per cent are paid for by the Department of Veterans Affairs and other sources. Among these are seven teaching hospitals and eight dedicated hospices and palliative care services. Overall the Catholic group employs about 30 000 people and represents 13 per cent of the whole sector. The church's contribution to the private health care makes up 25 per cent of the whole sector. While the bigger hospitals are in the capital cities, 23 of the 73 services are situated in larger rural centres including Wagga, Lismore, Bundaberg, Mackay, Launceston, Bendigo, Warrnambool, Bunbury and Geraldton.

The same pattern of decentralisation occurs in aged care, both in terms of geographic distribution and administration. Various Catholic organisations such as the religious orders, the Knights of the Southern Cross, the Saint Vincent de Paul Society, local parishes and others, provide almost 17 000 residential aged care beds, as well as just over 6000 retirement and independent living units. Increasingly, government policy is to try to deliver aged care at home through the Community Aged Care and Home and Community Aged Care Programs. The Catholic system provides almost 12 000 packages under these programs. Government funding, of course, is an essential part of all of these hospital and aged care services and, as we shall see, there is a fear that the church will be forced to conform to state, rather than Catholic, ministerial priorities. However, because it is such a large part of the system, governments are obliged to take the church's voice seriously.

Catholicism also has a sizeable overseas aid budget, most of it made up of donations from the community. For instance in 2005–06 $8 million was contributed through Project Compassion, an appeal to Catholics to contribute to aid programs as a Lenten penance. The overseas aid budget is administered through Caritas Australia, the local arm of Caritas Internationalis, Catholicism's world aid program. As in all of the church's work, aid is in no way tied to a religious test. 'Need' is the sole norm. Caritas Australia in 2005–06 raised $24.2 million, of which only $3.3 million came directly from the federal government through AusAID.[23] That is about $4.80 per year for every Catholic in Australia, whether attending church or not. This money was distributed to programs for Aborigines ($674 000) and East Timor ($954 000), as well as across south Asia ($2.2 million), east Asia ($2.4 million), the Pacific ($2.9 million), Africa ($2.9 million) and Latin America ($584 000). Eight-point-one million dollars was spent on emergencies like the tsunamis in Aceh and the Solomon Islands.

The two most extensive ministries that Australian Catholicism maintains are parishes and schools. Firstly parishes: the church operates 1363 local parishes throughout Australia although, due to the shortage of clergy, not all of them have a resident priest. These parishes are spread across 28 western-rite dioceses, four eastern-rite dioceses, and one covering the armed forces. They range in size from the largest in population terms, the archdiocese of Melbourne, with 226 parishes, to the dioceses of Darwin with 16 parishes, Geraldton with 12 and Broome with nine. But many of the country dioceses and parishes are vast in size with small, scattered populations. For instance the diocese of Geraldton with one bishop and 17 priests in parishes covers 1.318 million square kilometres and comprises one-seventh of Australia's land surface and is over twice the size of France. The diocese of Darwin at 1.295 million square kilometres is larger in area than South Africa, the western New South Wales diocese of Wilcannia–Forbes is one and a half times the size of the United Kingdom, and the diocese of Cairns is bigger than Germany. Parish

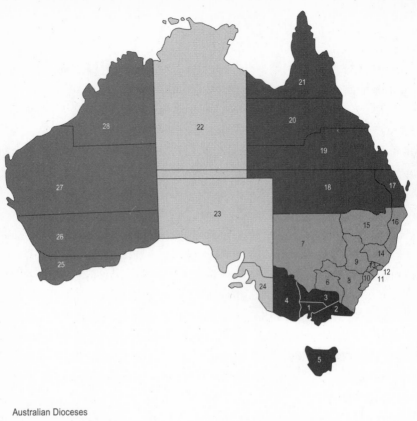

Australian Dioceses

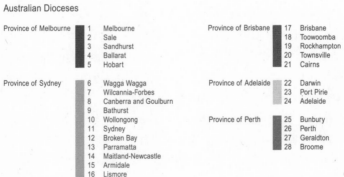

Province of Melbourne	1	Melbourne
	2	Sale
	3	Sandhurst
	4	Ballarat
	5	Hobart
Province of Sydney	6	Wagga Wagga
	7	Wilcannia-Forbes
	8	Canberra and Goulburn
	9	Bathurst
	10	Wollongong
	11	Sydney
	12	Broken Bay
	13	Parramatta
	14	Maitland-Newcastle
	15	Armidale
	16	Lismore

Province of Brisbane	17	Brisbane
	18	Toowoomba
	19	Rockhampton
	20	Townsville
	21	Cairns
Province of Adelaide	22	Darwin
	23	Port Pirie
	24	Adelaide
Province of Perth	25	Bunbury
	26	Perth
	27	Geraldton
	28	Broome

SOURCE *Official Directory of the Catholic Church in Australia*, 2007–2008. Map used with permission of the National Council of Priests of Australia Inc.

priests in these remote areas have to cover enormous distances: Broome, for instance, has only 11 priests, Townsville has 26 parishes and 19 priests with parochial appointments, and Port Pirie, which is three-and-a-half times the size of Italy, has 23 parishes and 21 active priests.[24]

Melbourne is by far the largest diocese with 992 000 Catholics, 30 per cent of the civil population of 3.3 million.[25] To give some sense of the reality of parish life in early 2007 I visited Hadfield which is a typical urban parish, on the flat, featureless northern side of Melbourne. It's a smallish suburb not far west of the Hume Highway heading north to Albury and Sydney. It is designed on a grid pattern and most of the well-maintained brick veneer and timber houses were built in the early 1960s. There are few trees, particularly natives, which is also typical of the northern suburbs.

The parish of Saint Thomas More was established in 1962 in the centre of the suburb. The 2001 census showed that Hadfield had a total population of 8000 of whom 3950, or 49.7 per cent, were Catholic.[26] Only 754 of the Catholics are under the age of 18, so this is an adult parish. Catholic primary school numbers are decreasing. The largest ethnic group is Italian–Australian with half the Catholic population of second or third generation Italian origin. The Maltese come second comprising 20 per cent of the parish, with smaller groups of Polish, East Timorese and Indians. There are also a number of Iraqi Catholics who attend the Chaldean Catholic church in nearby Campbellfield. This is a multicultural parish in the fullest sense.

The church is typical of the early 1970s: it is broad rather than elongated so that everyone can be reasonably close to the sanctuary. It is a plain, dark brick structure with an open sanctuary that embraces the whole church, a tabernacle behind the altar facing the people, a floor that inclines down toward the sanctuary and reasonably comfortable seats. The statues reflect the parish's ethnicity: Saint Anthony of Padua, Our Lady of Lourdes, Our Lady of Perpetual Succor and the Sacred Heart. The stylised wooden Stations of the Cross are very much 1970s period style.

The whole parish works as a community and Catholics have a sense of ownership and belonging. When asked why he presented himself for baptism a recent adult convert said that he 'loved the community' at Saint Thomas More. Ethnic suburbs with a strong Mediterranean cultural background like Hadfield still have a strong sense of family, clan and village and this works to assist the parish community. People know each other. Teamwork and co-operation is at the core of the parish's ministry. The parish priest is Father Emmanuel Bonello and the pastoral associate is Presentation Sister Michele Kennan. Together with the Parish Support Team (formerly the Parish Council), they focus primarily on pastoral care and keep across what is happening through reports from the different ministerial groups. As many people as possible are involved in the parish's various ministries. The parish has eight trained prayer leaders who can preside at Communion Services when the priest is absent and can give an effective reflection on the biblical text for the day.

There is also a Rite of Christian Initiation of Adults (RCIA) program, essentially a structured catechumenate or training program for those wishing to convert to Catholicism at Easter time. Some participants have already been baptised in another church, but many have not. Between 1992 and 2002 almost 48 000 people chose to become Catholics across Australia, an average of 4790 per year.[27] Some report that they were attracted by spirituality or the liturgy, but often the decision to convert was motivated by the experience of community, the feeling of being part of a welcoming group. One Hadfield parishioner who joined the local RCIA program says that as an adolescent he was angry with God when his grandfather died of cancer. 'I tried to fill the void in my life with drink, drugs and 'New Age' activities'. He 'hit rock bottom' when he left his partner in Melbourne suffering from post-natal depression and went to Cairns. It was there, after a bout of heavy drinking that he had a kind of spiritual experience of God's openness. 'I wasn't scared but felt oddly at peace for the first time in a long while.' He returned to Melbourne, his wife got through the depression 'and we were a family of three again. The days of excess are behind, as well as the other things I used to believe in.' Attending his wife's grandmother's funeral he was deeply moved by the Mass and finally 'realised what my calling was'. He discovered the RCIA group at the parish, joined and was received into the church on Easter Sunday. 'I realised that the void I had been trying to fill all those years was nothing compared to how I felt that day and have felt ever since.'[28]

Hadfield parish also has a trained bereavement team; with an aging population there are many funerals. Each team member is closely matched with the grieving family. The same kind of matching occurs in taking over 100 communions to the sick each week. The person bringing communion is asked to stay and talk with the house-bound, sick person. The three big nursing homes in the parish have a regular Celebration of the Word with Communion. The parish also runs a 'God Start' program which is a follow-up to baptism. Each year on the child's birthday a parishioner visits the family with a specially prepared card and the parish sponsors a birthday party for four-year-olds to introduce families to the Sunday school and the parish primary school.

One has the sense at Hadfield that while the priest and pastoral associate are central to the parish, they do not dominate it. At Saint Thomas More people say 'This is *our* parish' rather than 'This is Father so-and-so's parish'. Nevertheless Kennan and Bonello work extremely hard. They are on-call constantly and are lucky to get one day a week free: in the week prior to my visit Bonello said 16 Masses, a number of them funeral Masses, and that was considered a 'light week'. As the number of priests in Australia decrease and the average age rises, the pressure on those remaining is intense. Nevertheless in Hadfield there is a sense of understated efficiency, which no doubt comes from Michele Kennan's long experience as a school principal. The skillful use of computers has provided the parish with a tool for record keeping and for the preparation of worship, liturgy and information sheets.

Hadfield is part of the Broadmeadows Deanery which is co-ordinated by Bonello. The area houses a large Muslim population, particularly around Broadmeadows, and relations with the Islamic faith are an important part of the church's work. On an official level relationships are reasonably good, but that at the local level there are problems, not all rooted in racism. Many recently-arrived Muslims have difficulty relating to Australia and adapting to life here. On the other hand many Australians have trouble relating to a Muslim woman wearing a *burka*, a full or partial face mask; they compare it to a balaclava or ski mask. But people are trying: one man said that as a Lenten penance he 'smiled at a Muslim woman'. This may sound patronising, but at least it indicates good will. Whether she smiled back is unrecorded. The local Saint Vincent de Paul group assists many Muslims.

The secret to the success of Hadfield parish is that the ministry team and the parishioners try to pattern their lives on Jesus 'by being a welcoming community, open to the needs of one another … [and by striving] to embody the gospel values of Jesus Christ that lead us into service, worship and celebration' (Parish Vision Statement). Bonello says that this means that in pastoral care 'you don't create an obstacle course for people'. In other words Mass and the sacraments are there to provide grace and strength to help people live their lives as well as they can. *Sacramenta propter homines* is a basic theological principle: 'Sacraments are for people' and they should be made as widely available as possible without a whole accumulation of legalistic obstacles.

(Here I have to add that just after this book went to the publisher a change of personnel occurred at Hadfield. Father Bonello was moved by the archdiocese to another parish and a new priest, ordained in 2002, was appointed as administrator. His approach to parish ministry was very different to the approach described above and Sister Michele Kennan left soon afterwards.)

My second parish could not be more different. It is the combined rural parishes of Hughenden, Richmond and Winton in Townsville diocese in North-West Queensland. This is cattle country. It was once a vast inland sea and has produced a number of important fossils including the almost complete skeleton of a dinosaur. The area was first settled by whites in 1864. There is no money in sheep these days, but the cattle industry is doing well for the people on the stations, while those living in the towns make modest incomes working for local councils and Queensland Rail.

The local priest is Father Bill Brady. 'They call it the downs', he says.

> It was an inland sea. It's quite boring to drive in, straight roads with
> nothing to see … We're still in drought and it's totally barren, although
> we've had some rain and it does show some sign of recovery. However,
> people say they can make a good living out of it.[29]

He should know about the roads. 'Each weekend I drive 660 kilometres to cover three Masses. This week I had a couple of funerals and it all adds up to a bit more than that.' In fact in an 18-month period he covered 60 000 kilometres. He added that other priests in western Queensland drive even further.

This is sparsely settled country. Flinders Shire (of which Hughenden is the centre) has 2250 people and the town itself almost 1500. Richmond Shire has 1150 people and the town about 1000. Winton, famous as the place where Qantas began and where AB 'Banjo' Paterson composed *Waltzing Matilda*, has about 1200 people, most of them living in town. All up, a little over 4500 people living in an area approximately the size of the Republic of Ireland. These are people of purely Anglo–Celtic stock and they are generally politically conservative. 'There don't tend to be left wingers out here!' Brady says, laughing.

He is not alone in his ministry. There are two Good Samaritan Sisters in Hughenden, two Mercy Sisters in Winton, and a Josephite Sister at the Mary MacKillop House of Spirituality in Richmond. 'The sisters have a lot of rapport with the local people because they've been here for years, they work in the state schools, they visit people, especially the elderly, the hospitals and generally get around the place a lot more than I can because I'm on the move so much,' Brady says. 'They have a big impact.' There is certainly a high proportion of Catholics in the population, possibly up to a half, but only a small proportion are regular Mass-goers.

> The ones who are at Mass are very loyal and committed to the faith. They're the real survivors. They're very generous in their giving. When we have a parish council meeting the whole parish turns up. They're concerned with the pastoral work of the parish. They want to get people back to Mass.

Nevertheless people still get their children baptised even if they are not practising Catholics and they are committed to the parish's sacramental programs. Bill Brady is also often asked to do non-Catholic funerals as most people try to get a priest or minister for funerals.

Combined with constant driving, the biggest problem that priests face in these parishes is isolation and loneliness. Distance prevents much social life among the clergy. Brady's nearest priest neighbours are at Cloncurry almost 400 kilometres to the west and Charters Towers, 243 kilometres to the east.

Every couple of months priests do try to spend a week in Townsville for a break and to get back in touch with the broader church. For Brady this is an 800-kilometre round trip, but for his colleague further west at Mount Isa it is an 1840 kilometre round trip. Doug Conlan, who worked some years ago in a Western Australian country parish in the wheat belt, talks of the relentless travel in 'my hermitage-car' and 'the realisation that there were few, if any, in the bush with whom I could share my sometimes unbearable sense of loneliness'.[30]

The other key area of Catholic ministry in Australia is education. The church educates 19 per cent of all primary and 21 per cent of secondary students in Australia. In 2007, there were 686 000 students in 1646 schools, employing about 45 685 teachers and 14 700 non-teaching staff. Two-thirds of the teachers are women. Teacher/student ratios in Catholic schools are 1 to 18 students for primary and 1 to 13 students for secondary. A useful comparison is that in 1953 when I was in the first year of secondary school we had 80 students in one class. State schools educate 67 per cent of Australian primary and secondary students and other non-government schools educate 13 per cent. The federal government provides 53 per cent of funding for Catholic schools and state governments 19 per cent. This totals more than $4 billion annually, or about $5965 per student. The church itself provides 28 per cent of income through fees, borrowings and other sources.[31] About 77 per cent of students in Catholic schools come from at least nominally Catholic families and 23 per cent from non-Catholic homes. The National Catholic Education Commission (NCEC) notes

> this poses special questions for Catholic schools and their communities. Such questions concern the essential character and integrity of Catholic schools with large proportions of non-Catholic students; the expectations a school may have of students and parents; as well as pastoral implications. In summary, it touches on the tension between the Catholic school's evangelical and catechetical roles and aims.

About half of all Catholic families send their children to government schools.

Most of these come from the lower socio-economic bracket. There is also a small but growing group of upwardly-mobile Catholic students in other non-Catholic private schools. The NCEC notes that 'it is anticipated that there will be a trend for Catholics increasingly to select other non-government schools – especially for secondary education'. The report notes that low-income Catholic families tend to choose government schools while middle- and high-income Catholic families send their children to Catholic schools. 'A significant proportion of the richest Catholic households choose other non-government schools, presumably a high fee/high resource school.'[32]

A typical high school is MacKillop Catholic College, a co-educational school situated on two campuses (one catering for years seven to nine and the other 10 to 12) in the Tuggeranong Valley area of Canberra. As well as the original inner core of Canberra, the suburbs of the national capital are built around four town centres: Belconnen, Woden, Tuggeranong and Gungahlin. Tuggeranong is in a valley south of central Canberra towards the Brindabella Mountains. The population of Tuggeranong in 2004 was 89 829, with an average total income of $42 845. This is very much 'nappy valley' territory with 53.7 per cent of the population under 34. Only 5.5 per cent are over 65. The birth rate is 12.8 per thousand, against a death rate of 2.2 per thousand.[33] This is primarily a young, lower middle class area, populated mainly by lower-level public servants and trades persons, with the cheaper house prices that are typical of the edges of a large city. The housing stock is relatively new; the oldest houses date from the mid-1970s. There is a significant population of single-parent families and some people living in poverty. Quite a few live in heavy debt, often on cars (a necessity for mobility in Canberra with its inadequate public transport), or things like plasma TVs. The Saint Vincent de Paul Society report that many of the poor in the area have externally good homes, but have no furniture or food inside. Their poverty is hidden.

MacKillop Catholic College is the product of an amalgamation in 1998 of two schools.[34] Understandably there was resistance and tension given people's commitment to individual school communities, but now MacKillop, a co-educational school, has settled down and operates on two campuses a few kilometres apart. It is a large school with an enrolment of 1587 students in 2007. Of these, 56 per cent (893 students) were baptised Catholics, 248 were Anglicans, 54 said they were Christian, 47 Uniting, 34 Orthodox, 60 Protestant (Lutheran, Presbyterian, etc), 29 were non-Christians, and 211 said they had no religious affiliation. The school follows the enrolment policies of the Canberra–Goulburn archdiocese, which are typical of Australian dioceses.

> Those who choose a Catholic school for their children do so on the understanding that they respect and agree to support the Catholic identity of the school and acknowledge the importance of religious education for their children. The … school is open to all who are willing to support the philosophy, values and aims of Catholic schooling [Enrolment Policy Summary].

In practical terms this means that baptised Catholic children from a specific geographical area connected to the school get priority of admission, followed by Catholic children from outside the nominated area. Non-Catholic children are admitted if space is available and parents support the philosophy and values of Catholic education. All students are expected to participate in Religious Education (RE) classes and prayer and liturgy, as well as accept the emphasis on Catholic values.

Fee structures for Catholic systemic schools (that is schools that are part of the local diocesan system) are reasonable. In Canberra, parents would be expected to pay between $1000 and $1200 for the first child in primary school. MacKillop's 2007 annual fees ranged from $3879 in year seven to $4457 in year 12. This includes all levies and contributions. It compares very favourably with fee structures for elite private day schools that can range as high as $25 000 per year.

A little less than two-thirds of the teaching and support staff are Catholic. Before anyone, Catholic or non-Catholic, is employed as a teacher in a Catholic school they must agree to a 'statement of principles'; these are quite unequivocal.

Whilst [the Catholic school] is accountable to the community at large for the provision of quality education to young citizens, it is also accountable to the church community for providing this within the context of Christian gospel values as espoused by the Catholic tradition. The Catholic school is more than an educative institution; it is a key part of the church, an essential element in the church's mission … Teachers in Catholic schools are more than employees. They minister in the name of the church and of the Gospel … Only a person supportive of Catholic education philosophy may be a teacher in a Catholic school. Teachers bear witness to Christ and Christian values in their own lives and by personally supporting, evaluating, developing and disseminating the Catholic school philosophy.

This is a long way from the 'bad old days' in the mid-1970s when I used to visit a Catholic school in the parish where I was pastor to be treated with disdain by some teachers determined to tout their secularism. It was not personal; just contempt for Catholicism. So these principles are important because they emphasise the distinctiveness of Catholic education. The Catholic school is not a state school with RE thrown in as an extra. A Catholic–Christian ethos is essential to the core nature of a Catholic school and teachers have to reflect this in their lives. This ethos includes a sense of the sacred and spiritual, a participation in the Eucharist and worship, an espousal of Catholic moral values, a sense of justice and integrity, and a respect for the Catholic faith tradition.

In order to become an RE teacher, Canberra–Goulburn accreditation policies demand that staff need to be Catholics, to have at least a graduate diploma or degree in religious education and a consciousness that they 'are building on the foundations of faith expressed at baptism' and that they are 'Catholics with an on-going, demonstrable commitment to their own faith journey, the faith of the community and the Catholic tradition.' While non-Catholic teachers in the school often contribute an enormous amount to RE, 'they may not be formally responsible for a Religious Education class'. The emphasis on post-graduate study of RE is a big advance on the situation in the two and a half decades after 1970 when, as Paul Goonan, one of the

RE co-ordinators at MacKillop put it, 'All you needed was "Well, I went to a Catholic school".' In the 1990s the Canberra–Goulburn Catholic Education Office (CEO) pushed the idea of accreditation at diploma and degree levels and nowadays all Australian CEOs insist on qualifications to teach RE. As a result there is a shortage of RE teachers. Nevertheless, as Rita Daniels, principal at MacKillop pointed out, most Catholic schools would now insist on an RE qualification for promotion to senior positions in the Catholic system. This makes sense because you can hardly provide ministerial leadership if you don't have the experience, knowledge and qualification in the core subject in a Catholic school. Paul Goonan also made the point that RE teaching is not just knowledge; it needs to be linked to 'living Catholicism', to an integrated faith. Students are quick to discern disjunctions between theory and practise of the faith. So much of the success of the RE program depends on the teachers and their personal integration of faith and life.

The fact that Catholic students are at a Catholic school doesn't mean that they, or their parents, are in any way practising Catholics. Probably only 14 per cent would be regular Mass attendees. That is why schools like MacKillop have really moved from an emphasis on a catechetical to an evangelising model, that is they have shifted from an in-depth formation in Catholic belief to a more general Christian education with Catholic belief and practise integrated around that. They are almost forced to do this because they also have so many non-Catholic students and they have to draw everybody into the process. However, in the senior school, especially among the best students aiming for university entrance, there is much interest in the value of RE, which is studied with academic rigour. It is clear from MacKillop's syllabus that the historical, philosophical and sociological aspects of belief and faith are of great interest to intelligent senior students.

In the past there were often tensions between local parishes and systemic secondary schools which reported to the CEO. Local parish priests often saw these schools as thorns in their sides. Nowadays most of these problems have been ironed out. MacKillop, for instance, has a part-time school chaplain and the local parish priests are involved in Masses, liturgy and broader pastoral care. Mass is offered on campus once a week and attendance is voluntary. Personally, what impressed me most at MacKillop was that many of the laypeople running the school do have a genuine sense of ministry. They are there to care pastorally for their students, to nurture them personally toward an integrated humanity, as well as to support the beginning of faith and to challenge them to a deeper belief and spirituality.

MacKillop is an excellent illustration of the increasing role that laity play in ministry in Australian Catholicism. This was not so 50 years ago. Virtually all of the ministries of the church were run by sisters, brothers and priests who were paid at a subsistence level. Before state aid it was their poverty that made the Catholic school system viable. The statistics are revealing: in the four dioceses of Victoria in 1951 there were 2611 religious sisters and 356 brothers engaged in ministry, the vast majority teaching in schools, with a small percentage of the sisters in nursing and health care.[35] Their average age would have been probably less than 30. In the 2007–08 Catholic Directory there were 1551 sisters and 241 brothers listed in Victoria.[36] Only a tiny percentage of these are engaged in traditional ministries like health and education, and significantly their average age would be in the high 60s or early 70s. At the same time the number of students has increased three-fold. In 1951 when I went to the Christian Brothers' College, Victoria Parade, East Melbourne, only two of the teachers were laymen. The rest were brothers. At the time the school was about the same size as the average secondary school today with about 1000 or more students. In contrast, nowadays laypeople have stepped into the breach to replace the sisters and brothers almost completely.

This is a profoundly significant change that has only been made possible by 'state aid', that is government funding of Catholic schools, hospitals, health care facilities and charities. This has allowed a ministerial revolution in Catholicism to occur, because the church can now pay a proper living wage. Few other developed countries in the world would have so much lay involvement as Australia, but the key issue is lay formation and ongoing tertiary religious education for those working in ministry. The key question, of course, is whether this vast ministerial structure actually reflects the values and teachings of Christ and the tradition of Catholicism. For this to happen those ministering within the structure must reflect something of the goodness, generosity and commitment of Christ. They must also be committed to the church, the Eucharist, sacraments, prayer and the service of others. Without at least a proportion of committed Catholics and Christians working within these structures, their ministry will become little more than a kind of superficial religious window-dressing.

The other fact worth noting is that if you pool together all the church's work it is probably the second or third largest employer in Australia after the federal government. In other words this book is not about essentially small institutions such as the Pentecostal communities or other enthusiastic religious bodies that get extensive coverage in the media, but which ultimately have little or no impact on Australian life and culture. It is about the most significant and influential institution in the country after the federal government, and one which has been present in Australia since the beginning in 1788. Its influence is all the more pervasive because the media and chattering classes either don't notice it or choose to ignore it. In fact, as the next chapter shows, Catholics have extraordinary influence in contemporary Australian society.

2

Catholics in Australian society

In late July 2005 Benedict XVI went for his usual summer vacation to the Valle d'Aosta, a beautiful area north of Turin, just below the Great Saint Bernard Pass in the Italian Alps. He was chatting to a group of local clergy bemoaning the Western world's neglect of God and Christ. He spoke of the difficulty of believing and of the fact that 'the great churches seem to be dying'. And then he added, almost off the cuff: 'This is particularly true of Australia, also [of] Europe, but not so much in the United States.'[1] Why Australia was specifically targeted is hard to fathom. Since Benedict had never been to Australia this view of our 'Godlessness' must have been suggested to the Pope by someone. Perhaps one of the lesser lights among the Australian bishops had mentioned it during his quarter-of-an-hour interview with Benedict during his *ad limina* visit (diocesan bishops have to report to Rome personally every five years). Whatever the answer, it caused a minor media storm in Australia.

Mind you, it suits people, both secularists and churchmen, to maintain the notion that Australia is 'Godless' and the churches 'moribund'. For secularists it shows that they have been right all along. They can argue that denominational religion has always been a sectarian blight on Australian life. They say that if we all embraced a kind of 'one-religion-is-as-good-as-another' and 'who cares about unimportant doctrinal differences' and 'it's the same God we all worship' kind-of-approach, Australia would evolve into a tolerant, terrestrial paradise. This caricature still abounds, especially on the Left where religion is criticised for interference in politics accompanied by snide references to the crusades, the inquisition, the burning of witches and the wars of religion, often without the slightest notion of the complex history of these realities.

Although this should not be over-emphasised, an understated, but pervasive, anti-Catholic and anti-Christian feeling sometimes bubbles to the surface in Australia. You see anti-Catholicism in the comments made about Catholics that you would never hear made about other religions. The disdain shown towards the churches by the former Labor leader Mark Latham reminds us that aggressive secularism is alive and well in some parts of the Australian Labor Party (ALP). Lumping all the mainstream churches and fundamentalist sects together Latham says that the 'first law of the church' is 'the greater the degree of fanaticism in so-called faith, the greater the degree of escapism either from addiction (alcohol, drugs, gambling or sex) or from personal tragedy ... Organised religion: just another form of conservative command and control in our society.'[2] In a lecture at Melbourne University Latham spoke about the 'weirdos of the religious right, with their sexual hang-ups and policy obsessions'. By usual Labor standards, these views are extreme. But he is not alone. Greens Senator Kerry Nettle showed similar contempt in February 2006 during the debate on the abortion drug RU486, when she wore a T-shirt with the caption 'Mr Abbott, Get you rosaries off my ovaries'. Interestingly the T-shirt originated with the Young Women's Christian Association, a para-Christian group rooted in the Protestant tradition. In the course of the debate Nettle told the *Sydney Morning Herald* (10/2/06) that 'Religion has no place in politics.'

By contrast, church leaders use Australian Godlessness to claim that the collapse in religious belief and practise isn't really their fault. Its not church structures, poor leadership, dull sermons, uninspired ministry, lifeless worship or failure to address the real issues facing contemporary society that has led so many people to abandon the church. It is all really the fault of the materialism and relativism of the unwashed punters. It's society that has to change, not justified and righteous church leaders.

I would have thought it difficult to argue convincingly that Australia is the *most* secular place in the world. Certainly parts of Europe could make a strong claim, including Benedict's own Germany, or France, where Catholicism has suffered long-term declines. Australians are not crass materialists, nor are they secular, lazy beach-loving slobs. And the local branch of Catholicism, while it may be seriously ill, is not yet in its terminal stages. Benedict XVI's perceptions about Australian 'Godlessness' may be explained by the fact that our religiosity is non-dogmatic, egalitarian and simply doesn't take institutional authority seriously. Australians are independent, sceptical and laid back. What we don't agree with, we ignore. This doesn't mean that we are not spiritual in understated ways, and we can be surprisingly reverent in unexpected places, like the bush. All the evidence suggests that there is a strong belief in the transcendent; this is especially true of those who are in touch with our extraordinary landscape.

Professor Gary Bouma of Monash University in his *Australian Soul* agrees that Australians are quietly spiritual, rather than explicitly religious, holding what historian, Manning Clark, called 'a shy hope in the heart'. Bouma says that Australian spirituality is understated, and ultimately characterised by 'a serious quiet reverence, a deliberate silence … an inarticulate awe and a serious distaste for glib wordiness'.[3] He claims that part of the problem is that we tend to judge ourselves by the ostentatious religiosity of American Protestantism. He has argued for two decades, that belief is not marginal to Australian life and that the large majority of Australians have usually thought of themselves as believers.[4] David Millikan in his ABC TV documentary and book *The Sunburnt Soul* argued in a similar vein in 1981 that Australians are 'looking for a form of religious expression which is sensitive to the spirit this land has within it. Australia has a vast and silent spiritual heart … experienced by almost everyone who has been there'. In an astute aside Millikan adds that 'we have not yet been able to tune our ears to the sound of its voice'.[5] Throughout the 20th century, and especially after the 1960s, the predominant view among the chattering classes was that Australia was an explicitly secular society and that meaning questions would all eventually be solved by science. This is still reflected in the mainstream media. Certainly there is a growing group of people in Australia who place themselves in the 'no religion' category in the census. In 1996 this group was 16.6 per cent of the population and rose to 18.7 per cent or 3.7 million people in the 2006 census, exactly the same percentage of the population as identify with the Anglican church. But whether these are 'hardcore' secularists is debatable. However, the no religion category is still outnumbered four-to-one by those who state a religious commitment.[6]

In some ways the 'no religion' response is typically Australian. People are not looking for simple answers, they don't need a religious authority to tell them what to do and they are especially suspicious of institutions 'with all the answers'. They are more content to live with the questions and they certainly want to take charge of their own spiritual lives. In ecclesiastical terms the groups that are growing are 'oriental Christian' (that is the Orthodox growing largely due to migration) and 'other Christian'. Bouma says 'The 'other Christian' category includes many independent congregations and small groups of congregations. Some of these provide a charismatic worship style and conservative, family-oriented ethos. In this they are similar to the Pentecostals.'[7] He points out that the mainstream Anglican, Uniting and Protestant churches are in decline. The Anglicans lost 4.7 per cent of their membership between the 1996 and 2006 censuses. The Uniting and Presbyterian and Reformed churches are facing even higher decreases: between 1996 and 2006 the Uniting Church dropped 14.9 per cent (that is from 1.3 million to 1.1 million and the Reformed churches 11.7 per cent (that is from 675 000 to 596 000).[8] With parallel declines in New Zealand, Canada and the USA, Bouma claims that 'this represents the waning of British Protestantism'.[9] Protestantism has been, to some extent, successful where it has moved toward the evangelical end of the spectrum, although according to Bouma, Sydney Anglicans, who have done exactly that, actually declined by 10.5 per cent in the 2006 census.[10]

Bouma, however, is quite optimistic about Catholicism, which he sees as being in a different position. While he concedes that there have been decreases in attendance and that Catholics have much larger parishes with a very high priest to people ratio, he thinks the school system and strong institutions will sustain the church. He points out that increasingly non-Catholic parents want to enrol their children in Catholic schools because of the discipline and values-based education that they offer. Another Anglican, Dr Ian Markham, in a recent paper also argued that religion will thrive and Catholicism will prosper in the 21st century. He says that secular humanism historically is 'a cultural aberration' that has already failed, although it is 'disproportionately influential in the media and some of our public institutions'.[11] He says: 'In my view Roman Catholicism concludes this [20th] century in remarkably good shape, despite the tensions and decline in many parts of Europe. It remains the largest Christian (and therefore the largest religious) community in the world.'[12]

I would be more cautious about Australian Catholicism's future. Certainly all of the evidence shows that in many places, especially Africa and parts of Asia, the church is growing and will prosper, and there is no doubt that it will be a major force in the 21st-century world. However, this doesn't mean that Catholicism in specific places, like Europe or Australia, might not be in trouble. The more optimistic picture is re-enforced by the fact that from 1947 to 2001 there was an almost 6 per cent increase in the Catholic population in Australia, although this was almost entirely due to post-war immigration, not to fertility. In the 1986 census Catholics became the largest religious community in Australia with 26.1 per cent of the population. It was 27.3 per cent in 1991 and in 2001 Catholic numbers reached 5 001 624 or 26.6 per cent, a slight drop in proportional terms in relationship to the whole population. In the 2006 census the Catholic proportion declined again to 25.8 per cent because the national population was growing faster due to high rates of immigration. But the number of Catholics also increased between 2001 and 2006 by 125 000 to 5 126 900, a 2.5 per cent growth. This is entirely due to immigration because Catholic fertility is now marginally below the national fertility rate.

This gives the lie to the accusation that Australian Catholics have always had lots of children. There is a story told by Dame Enid Lyons of an exchange between her husband, the then Australian prime minister, Joseph Aloysius Lyons, a Catholic, and the Northern Ireland prime minister, the rabid

Orangeman Lord Craigavon, at the Imperial Conference in London in May 1937. Craigavon was 'fiercely anti-Catholic' and

> knowing nothing of Joe's background had asked him at a banquet, 'Lyons, have you got many Catholics in Australia?' 'Oh, about one in five', Joe had replied. 'Well watch 'em, Lyons, watch 'em,' Craigavon had urged. 'They breed like bloody rabbits!'

The Australian prime minister's response was not recorded, but he and Enid had six daughters and five sons and they were both practising Catholics![13]

No doubt the size of the Lyons' family would have re-enforced the notion that Australian Catholic fertility was much higher than the national average. However, the historical evidence shows that this is a caricature. Even the Catholic preoccupation with sex is a relatively modern phenomenon. In the 18th century and for most of the 19th there was little focus on sexual and reproductive issues among Catholic moralists, or by priests at the parochial level, or in statements from the pope or the Vatican. The 19th century clergy in Australia were more concerned with the problems of drunkenness, violence, religious ignorance, and the tendency to abandon the church in order to gain economic or social preferment.[14]

Throughout this period birth rates were high for everyone, Catholic and Protestant alike. For instance, Australian women born between 1840 and 1855 would have borne at least seven children on average, with 20 per cent having 11 or more. Also the infant mortality rate was high, with 104 babies per thousand dying before their first birthday.[15] Catholics and Protestants only became involved in reproductive issues from about 1870 onwards with the emergence of the birth-control movement, the declining birth rate and an increased medical focus on sexuality. Senior US judge and author John T Noonan says 'A vigorous attack on birth control began only in the last quarter of the nineteenth century' in the Catholic church.[16] At this time mechanical contraceptive devices became more widely accepted. By the time of Federation in 1901 there was moral panic in Australia about the fall in the birth rate, the presumed danger of 'race suicide' and the fear of being overrun by Asian hordes. This led to a 1903 New South Wales Royal Commission on *The Decline of the Birth-Rate*. Only one woman gave evidence. According to the commissioners 'female selfishness' was to blame and they waxed eloquent about the dangers of birth control. Having as many children as fertility determined was 'natural'; birth control was 'unnatural'.[17] All of this influenced the clergy of all churches and re-enforced the view among Catholic priests that any form of contraception was against the natural law. Parallel with the concern about contraception, the medical profession became increasingly preoccupied with masturbation and coitus interruptus. These practises were said to cause neuroticism and insanity.

However, the moral panic engendered by the Royal Commission did nothing to halt the fall in the birth rate. Women who reached child-bearing age in 1911 on average had four children or less.[18] Dr Anne O'Brien makes the important observation that 'For all women, church teachings existed alongside a range of political, educational and social influences, but the most important factor determining their choice was economic survival.'[19] In a detailed analysis of Australian fertility between 1891 and 1931 Hans Mol, in his classic study *Religion in Australia*, shows that Catholics had less children per fertile woman than Protestants and others. However, Mol argues that Catholics also had a larger number of unmarried women, and if these are subtracted from the equation, Catholic fertility is marginally higher than that of the total population.[20]

Mol's approach is an artificial way of looking at the census. The number of unmarried women must be part of the fertility figures, since they are able to bear children but for whatever reason have decided against it. Historically Catholics hovered around the national fertility average, or even slightly below it. If you take the years 1901 (Federation) to 1947 (the beginning of post-war immigration), the total population grew from 3.7 million to 7.5 million. During that same period, when immigration was negligible and almost all increases depended on fertility, the Catholic proportion of the population actually dropped almost 2 per cent. If some Catholics had big families like Enid and Joe Lyons, so did many other Australians. This throws doubt on the notion that Australian Catholics were priest-ridden sheep who did whatever they were told by the clergy. All of the evidence points to the fact that ordinary Catholics have always made up their own minds about important issues like fertility. As O'Brien emphasises economic factors would have been the decider. A possible case might be made that for a couple of decades around World War II Catholics did follow the Vatican teaching. But once the contraceptive pill became available they returned in droves to making up their own minds.

It would also be interesting to know how often they were harangued from the pulpit about birth control. Certainly the 'militant prudery' of a prelate like Michael Kelly, archbishop of Sydney from 1911 to 1940, was not taken seriously by many Catholics. As historian, Patrick O'Farrell notes:

> Some rejected the official line with bitter resentment. Others, more healthily, took it with a grain of salt: beneath the elevated world of Kelly's scrupulous shunning of subjects sexual, was an ordinary – sometimes crude – Catholic populace which found his strictures of little relevance and sometimes funny.[21]

From the late 1960s onward, with the ready availability of the contraceptive pill, Catholics remained firmly in tandem with general reproduction rates. Nowadays Catholic fertility is actually slightly lower than that of the rest of the population: Catholics have 1.3 per cent less children aged four or under than the national average. At the same time Catholic labour force participation is higher and they earn more: $900 per week compared to the national average of $740. Seventy per cent of Catholics own their own home and the church is the most ethnically diverse community in Australia.

As the new millennium begins, Catholics are to be found throughout public life. For a period in the mid-1990s the three most powerful men in the country, the prime minister (Paul Keating), the governor-general (Sir William Deane) and the chief justice (Sir Gerard Brennan) were all self-confessed Catholics. Catholics are very prominent in the law although these days less apparently so in the medical profession. They are also numerous in theatre and media: for instance actor Nicole Kidman, broadcasters Geraldine Doogue and Bert Newton, poets Les Murray and Bruce Dawe, novelists the late Morris West and Tom Kenneally, singer-songwriter, Paul Kelly and newspaper mogul Rupert Murdoch (a convert) are all well-known Catholics. The senior ranks of the armed forces are now decidedly Catholic-friendly: former chief of the Defence Force, Peter Cosgrove, and present head of the army, Peter Leahy, are both Catholics. At one stage in the late-1990s almost all the generals in the Australian army were not only Catholics, but graduates of Christian Brothers' colleges. Many former and present state premiers are Catholics, as are many prominent police-persons.

Perhaps my preoccupation with who is a Catholic and who is not is indicative of my age and interests! Many younger people nowadays couldn't care less whether someone was a Catholic or not. Denominational differences are rarely taken very seriously, although many people are still interested in whether someone is religious or not.

Nevertheless historically, Catholics were wedded to the Labor Party, which represented their working class economic status and aspirations. The Liberal Party was seen as the stronghold of the Protestant and Anglican establishment. The Liberals made little effort to enlist Catholics and few joined. Sectarianism was part of the problem and quite a few local branches of the Liberal Party were opposed to recruiting Catholics. This neglect was based more on snobbery than sectarianism. Among the few prominent Catholics in the Liberal Party were Dame Enid Lyons and Sir John Cramer, a founder of the Liberal Party. He held Sydney's north shore seat of Bennelong from 1949 to 1974. His successor was John Howard. Even when many Catholics voted Liberal in the 1949 federal election because of their anti-Communist stance, nothing was done to maintain this Catholic vote. In the Fraser years (1975–83) there were only a few Catholics in the ministry, like Fred Chaney and Phillip Lynch. Political scientist John Warhurst points out that the bond between Catholic and Labor has now been broken, and Catholics are found on all sides of the parliament. The change occurred remarkably quickly from the 1990s onwards, and nowadays Catholics are just as likely to vote for the Coalition as they are to vote Labor.[22] At least 15 ministers and parliamentary secretaries out of 43 in the fourth Howard ministry were Catholics including Tony Abbott whose nickname 'the mad monk' pointed to both his Catholicism and the fact that he had trained for the priesthood although, of course, he had never been ordained.

The fact that Catholics have become swinging or 'aspirational' voters shows that the tacitly-understood (but never publicly articulated) project of getting Catholics out of the working class ghetto and into the mainstream has been successful. Throughout the last half of the 20th century, largely as a result of Catholic schools and religious orders like the Christian Brothers trying to lift their students through secondary education beyond the status of their working class parents, Catholics have 'made it' economically and socially into the mainstream.

Aspirationals typically live in the outer suburbs of our capital cities with a high level of personal debt. They have nought to three children and have borrowed heavily to purchase houses since interest rates fell. Haydon Manning of Flinders University says they have been 'variously described as the new "conservative right" – anti-egalitarian and anti-union, favouring tax cuts ... and sending their kids to private schools'.[23] Manning has shown that a high proportion of them (up to 70 per cent) vote Liberal and that they helped to shore up the Coalition's vote across Australia's outer suburbs throughout the Coalition ascendency from 1996 to 2007. It is a reasonable supposition that perhaps 25 per cent of aspirationals are Catholics. A proportion of these Catholics are recent arrivals from countries like India, Burma, Mauritius, Malaysia and other countries where Catholics, who are often members of the professional middle class or qualified tradespeople, are very much a discriminated-against minority and emigration is an attractive option.

In the past, Labor usually had up to a third or more of Catholic members in the parliamentary ranks. However, as a result of the bitter 1950s 'split' when many Catholics left the party to form the Democratic Labor Party (DLP), especially in Victoria, Queensland and Tasmania, the Labor tradition has started being much more discreet about publicising religious affiliation. The DLP kept Labor out of office for 20 years, and without a doubt supporting the DLP made it easier for former ALP voters to cross the Rubicon and vote Liberal. Also there has always been a numerically strong humanist-secularist influence in Labor ranks, whose influence increased with the departure of Catholics to join the DLP. Nevertheless, Prime Minister Kevin Rudd is probably the parliament's best-known Christian. He was born and brought up a Catholic, but nowadays attends a Brisbane Anglican church and calls himself a 'non-denominational Christian'.

Unlike the United States, there has never been a complete separation of church and state in Australia, but the tendency historically has been for politicians to downplay their religion. What is new and striking these days is that it has become a badge of honour for many politicians to tout their religion publicly. As John Warhurst has pointed out the Howard government more than any other federal administration was 'active, in word and deed in emphasizing (or at least being open about) its religious credentials and beliefs and in emphasizing the positive contribution of Christian values to Australian society'.[24] Commentator Brian Toohey has noted that the proportion of politicians who publicly espouse Christianity is much higher than the national average.[25] This is shown by the number of politicians who are members of the Parliamentary Christian Fellowship: it's hard to get exact figures but possibly between 60 and 75 belong to this group and most come from Coalition ranks.[26] Many in the Fellowship tend to wear their faith on their sleeve, although Catholic members are usually more low-key about their religious affiliation.

The problem is that some Christian politicians (on the Coalition side especially) have a tendency to identify Christianity with their own (often evangelical, or Assemblies of God, or fundamentalist) version of faith. These people are very up-front in promoting a morality focused mainly on a gender and sexuality. At the same time they ignore broader ethical issues embedded in the selfish materialism of neo-capitalist economics, while arguing the moral justification of things such as invading Iraq. As Dr Marion Maddox, author of

God Under Howard (2005) pointed out, they don't actually use explicitly theological language. She told the *Sunday* program (3 July 2005):

> It's safer to keep religion out of the overt language you use, so instead of talking about sin or salvation or damnation … it's safer to talk about family or tradition or heritage or values … those sorts of terms … have become a kind of secular shorthand.

The Family First Party, which originated in the Assemblies of God, use a rhetoric focused on the nuclear family as their way of influencing public policy. With the election of a Family First senator from Victoria in 2004, albeit because of a preferential deal with the apparatchicks of the Victorian ALP to exclude the Greens, there is a feeling that large numbers of people out there support these groups.

But we need to keep a clear statistical perspective. They ultimately represent few people and have a disproportionate influence. Because constant media emphasis is placed on their increasing numbers and television images show vast crowds, many assume they will soon outnumber the mainstream churches. But the 1996 census showed that they only made up about 1 per cent of the population with a total of about 174 000 people involved.[27] This has increased in the last six years to 219 000 or 1.1 per cent of the population.[28] Even if we allow that up to half of the 'other Christian' category (776 900 or 3.9 per cent of the population in the 2006 census) belong in the fundamentalist or Pentecostal camps, at most they still only constitute about half a million or about 3.2 per cent of the population.

Nevertheless this seems to have freed Kevin Rudd to depart from the usual Labor reticence about religion. His first foray was his much-discussed 'Faith in Politics' article in *The Monthly*.[29] Here he is particularly scathing about those politicians who say 'Vote for me because I'm a Christian, and because I have a defined set of views on a narrowly defined set of questions concerning sexual morality.' Rudd rightly says:

> I see very little evidence that this pre-occupation with sexual morality is consistent with the spirit and content of the gospels. For instance there

is no evidence of Jesus ... expressly preaching against homosexuality. In contrast there is considerable evidence of ... [Jesus] preaching against poverty and the indifference of the rich.

He highlights the role religion plays in forming attitudes to social justice and public morality. He emphasises that Christian ethics means nothing without social action, and this in turn has political implications. His hero is Dietrich Bonhoeffer, and for Rudd the martyred German Lutheran pastor, who was killed by the Nazis in the last weeks of the war, stands for an engaged faith that is involved with the outcasts and defenceless. He argues that the disciple of Jesus must speak out about injustices and suffer the consequences, which occasionally will involve crucifixion. The church belongs not in the sacristy sheltering from the world and supporting a privatised faith, but in the middle of life 'as a counterculture operating within what some have called a post-Christian world'. This means that Christianity 'must always take the side of the marginalised, the vulnerable and the oppressed ... women, gentiles, tax collectors, prostitutes and the poor'. This tradition draws on the prophetic literature of the Hebrew Scriptures and the teaching of the gospels.

On the question of economic self-interest and the massive accumulation of private wealth, Rudd comments that 'we are left with the troubling parable' where Jesus says that it would be easier for a camel to pass through the eye of a needle than for the rich to be saved. But he balances this with a reference to Catholic social teaching on the 'proper balance between the rights of capital and labour, in a relationship based on mutual respect as well as legal protection'. Here is the essential basis for his approach on industrial relations. Rudd also points out that the Christian moral teaching on just war 'is anchored in the Christian concern for the sanctity of all human life ... Human life can only be taken in self-defence, and then only under highly conditional circumstances ... and if war is to be embarked upon then the principles of proportionality must apply.' Here he refers specifically to Pope John Paul II and the Vatican's total opposition to the pre-emptive invasion of Iraq as a just war.

In another article entitled 'Howard's Brutopia' Rudd's argument is much more directly political.[30] Here he points to the ethical inconsistency between the Coalition's emphasis on traditional social values of family, community and country and their parallel emphasis on 'the ruthless economic utilitarianism of a market in which rampant individualism is dominant'. As he says 'there is nothing sentimental about unrestrained self-interest'. He argues that contemporary Liberals have abandoned the socially responsible liberalism that characterised Coalition prime ministers from Robert Menzies to Malcolm Fraser, and embraced an extreme form of Thatcherite neo-liberalism, which is based on the unremitting pursuit of wealth and money in a world which favours the survival of the fittest. This type of economic fundamentalism was advocated by the guru of limitless material acquisition, Friedrich von Hayek, who explicitly excluded social justice, community solidarity, generosity and altruism in favour of the absolute rights of private property and rampant capitalism. Rudd argues persuasively that 'the relentless march of market fundamentalism' and individualism will inexorably swallow-up and destroy the families, communities and even the nation itself.

Ultimately what Rudd did is articulate a vision which spells out how the Centre–Left of politics might begin to realise the Christian vision of social justice in terms of practical politics. He wants to counter the claim of Coalition and other conservative politicians that they have a monopoly on Christian faith and that their vision exhausts the teaching of Jesus and the social tradition of the church. But once he became party leader his essential conservatism began to manifest itself. As the 24 November 2007 election approached he showed a ruthless *realpolitik* that was willing to sacrifice ideals to the demands of getting elected. For instance, it became almost impossible before the election to differentiate Rudd from Howard on economic questions. They were in lock-step also on most questions focusing on the environment as Labor's support for the Tasmanian pulp mill and for old-growth logging demonstrated. Labor was only marginally better than the Coalition on the issue of global warming.

However, this whole ethical debate is entirely new in terms of Australian politics, and takes us far from the rather bland secularism of the Fraser–Hawke–Keating years. It gives Catholicism a chance to reclaim a genuine place in the national dialogue about the meaning of life in Australia and of the ethics that govern it. More significant in the long-term than Rudd's social theology was an important article by Clive Hamilton of The Australia Institute in *Eureka Street*, entitled 'Churches could Hold the Key to Salvation for the Left'.[31] Hamilton argues that in the past the Left evolved to confront capitalism and deal with the material deprivation of the working class. He pointed out that nowadays it is not so much deprivation that we face, but the consequences of our 'affluenza': over-consumption, wastefulness, materialism, selfishness, and loss of meaning. 'Now that most people in rich countries have conquered material deprivation', Hamilton says, 'we see a rash of psychological disorders and a pervasive emptiness in everyday life'. He points out that there are still many progressives in the Christian churches, particularly in Catholicism with its strong social justice tradition. He suggests that Catholics may offer a way forward for the progressive Left, nowadays marginalised by the dominance of neo-liberalism and the kind of social conservatism that characterises the Labor Right including Rudd. Hamilton asks 'What social movement or popular yearning could generate [progressive] ... politics in an affluent society characterised by a profound loss of meaning?' His surprising answer is: the churches, and particularly Catholicism!

Hamilton admits that progressives are suspicious of Catholicism because of the emphasis on sexual morality and the failure to support gender issues, for example legalised relationships for gay people. 'Usually progressives regard this as a dangerous thing, because the most newsworthy stories concern sexual and reproductive questions where the churches often line-up against the progress made by the liberation movements of the '60s and '70s.' Nevertheless he argues that 'Traditionally, the churches have attended to and represented the deeper aspects of life, those that transcend the individualism, materialism and selfishness that so characterise modern affluent societies.' He sees the religious communities offering a foundation for a morality for contemporary society and providing an antidote to post-modernism, which, he says, 'has no metaphysical foundation for a moral critique'. 'After all', he continues, 'every political debate is a moral debate'. This is especially true of debates about economics. Hamilton argues strongly that the Left needs to try to find a moral ground that spans both their traditional concern with social justice and with moral issues concerning personal behaviour. What the Rudd and Hamilton articles have shown is that debate about belief and moral issues is not dead in Australia and that the churches, particularly the Catholic church, are finding a reinvigorated voice and are willing to participate in discussions about these questions.

In that context it is important to ask: How much 'conservative command and control', as Mark Latham called it, does the Catholic church wield in Australian society? Actually, not much! As successive Howard governments vividly showed, the fact that there are a lot of Catholics in power does not mean that somehow the church will able to realise its ethical agenda. It has certainly not been successful in any of its moral 'crusades'. For instance John Warhurst pointed out that Catholicism has always been firmly opposed to market-dominated economic rationalism.

> While generally unsuccessful and often unacknowledged, the church has been one of the last traditional institutions to resist the allure of the economic nostrums of the right … The Catholic lobby broadly defined (bishops, agencies and prominent individual priests and laypeople) has loudly criticised many social, economic and foreign policies to which the government and (to a large extent) the Opposition have been committed.[32]

Benedict XVI has taken up the same theme. Opening the Latin American Bishops' Conference in Brazil on 13 May 2007 he predictably condemned Marxism, but went on to warn of the dangers of unfettered capitalism and globalisation. He pointed out that the fruits of capitalism are a growing divide between rich and poor and 'a worrying degradation of personal dignity through drugs, alcohol and deceptive illusions of happiness'.[33] Nevertheless the church has had no success in persuading even Catholic politicians to adopt its critique of neo-rationalist economics.

But this is not the only area where Catholicism has had no success. Take the issue of therapeutic cloning. After passing the Senate by a narrow margin in November 2006, a private member's Bill which allowed scientists to clone and use embryos for research for up to 14 days, went to the House of Representatives and was passed easily on 6 December 2006 in a conscience vote. While there was opposition to the Bill from the bishops and distinguished Catholic ethicists like Jesuit Father Bill Uren, there were a number of Catholic politicians who voted for it. Among them were Liberal ministers Brendan Nelson and Joe Hockey, who referred explicitly to his Catholic faith and Jesuit formation at secondary school, but who still conscientiously voted for the Bill, as did Michael Hatton, former Labor member for Blaxland, who gave a detailed speech to explain his position, again highlighting the question of conscience.[34]

Among those who opposed the Bill were John Howard and Kevin Rudd. Both referred to their Christian background.[35] In a carefully balanced speech, Rudd referred to his mother who had died in 2004 from Parkinson's disease, an illness that some claimed might be cured by research based on therapeutic cloning. He described her as 'a Catholic from central casting' who, when he asked her advice on a similar Bill in 2002 said: 'In the great traditions of the Church, Kev, that is a question for your conscience, not mine.' What influence, if any, should the churches have on ethical debate? 'I have said before that the Christian churches are as entitled to engage in this debate as anyone else in the community.' But he warned that the churches 'do not have a monopoly when it comes to questions of ethics. Fundamental ethical questions can be shaped by a range of theological and philosophical traditions'. He made the point that he found it 'difficult to support a legal regime which allows creation of a form of human life with the single purpose of allowing the conduct of experimentation on that form of human life … I am concerned about the crossing of such an ethical threshold and where it might lead in the long term.'[36] This is precisely the position of Father Uren and the Catholic church. But despite the opposition of both the then prime minister and leader of the Opposition, the Bill passed.

Clearly, the church is far from getting its own way in 'moral crusades'. When similar Bills came before the Western Australian and New South

Wales' parliaments Cardinal George Pell and Archbishop Barry Hickey tried less subtle approaches than Bill Uren. They threatened Catholic politicians with un-named 'penalties'. Hickey quickly backed down when threatened with an appearance before the Parliamentary Privileges Committee and Pell was roundly criticised by Catholic parliamentarians, the media and the broader public. It revealed the essential weakness of a boots and all approach.

The debate over climate change has also re-introduced the discourse of morality and ethics into politics. At his climate change summit in early April 2007 Kevin Rudd said it was the 'great *moral* challenge of our generation', although this didn't prevent him after becoming ALP leader from supporting the further destruction of an important natural carbon sink: Tasmania's old growth forests to get votes in marginal seats. Greens' Senator Christine Milne had beaten Rudd to the punch when in November 2006 she quoted George Monbiot arguing that climate change 'is the moral question of the twenty-first century'. In rhetoric that reflected her Catholic background, Milne said that climate change 'goes to the heart of questions of justice, equity and the survival of human kind and the ecosystems on which all life depends. These are the values that need to be brought to the question'. She assured the Senate that 'There is one position even more morally culpable than denial. This is to accept that it's happening and that its results will be catastrophic; but to fail to take the measures needed to prevent it. The Howard government stands condemned.'[37] The best response Howard could muster was to say that there were 'other challenges with moral dimensions just as real and pressing as those which surround climate change', but this was before his climate change 'conversion' as he struggled for re-election.[38]

Where Catholicism has been most successful with both Coalition and Labor governments has been in obtaining support for Catholic education, schools, hospitals, health care, institutions and other ancillary services that the church runs. As Amanda Lohrey said in her Quarterly Essay *Voting for Jesus*:

the churches have been remarkably successful in lobbying for an economic agenda that is straight-forwardly about maximising government funding of the churches' own infrastructure through tax exemptions, along with direct subsidy in the areas of education and welfare. This … relies on a canny electoral blackmail that has nothing to do with moral crusades.[39]

While I am not certain about the 'electoral blackmail' given that there is no such thing as a 'Catholic vote' these days, it is true that Australian church officials know precisely when to get off the moral high horse and negotiate *realpolitik* with governments of both persuasions.

However, Catholicism's bargaining power has to be seen within the context of the extraordinary extent of its contribution to the educational, social, health, welfare and the human service sectors in Australia. Certainly these days much of the funding comes from government and there is always the real danger that the church's ministry will be subsumed by political priorities, which are sometimes different to the church's. The other acute danger is that the Christian motivation of these services will be drowned in a generic desire to 'do good'. Secular professionalism may replace ministerial service, which reflects the sheer generosity of God and strong commitment to the poorest in society. Nevertheless, the range and extent of Catholicism's service sector gives it a strength and impetus which is largely unacknowledged.[40]

The role of Catholicism in Australia is unique in the English-speaking world. There is nothing similar in the US where, decades ago, Catholic primary and secondary education collapsed as a result of the failure to gain state aid for church schools. Catholic health care there has been largely privatised, although welfare services are still supported by the church community. In the UK there is state support for church schools, with about 10 per cent of all students (839 000) in Catholic systemic schools, as well as 130 independent fee-paying schools. Three Canadian provinces (Ontario, Alberta and Saskatchewan) fund Catholic education in a similar way to Australia.

Nevertheless some politicians state that the church should retire to the sacristy. We have already seen the views of former Senators Lyn Allison (Democrats) and Kerry Nettle (Greens) who want religion kept out of politics. Allison has argued that decreasing church attendance and 'the fact that more Australians than ever profess no religious beliefs' or are non-Christians, means that religion should be relegated to the margins of society. She concedes that the church should have a voice, but says that 'the growing presence of religion ... compromises democracy, undermining commitment to freedom, equality and tolerance'.[41] Part of the problem with her argument is her tendency to lump all religions together as if they were all the same. And there is the usual historical amnesia that forgets that Anglicanism, Protestantism and Catholicism are not new arrivals here; they are part of the fabric of Australian history, culture and democracy.

Howard government foreign minister, Alexander Downer, also weighed into this argument in the Sir Thomas Playford Annual Lecture in August 2003. Downer's main target was the then Anglican Primate, Archbishop Peter Carnley, and the just-retired president of the Uniting Church, Reverend Professor James Haire. Downer, an Anglican, attacked Carnley because the archbishop had said that the Bali bombing resulted from Australia's close alliance with the US. The foreign minister conceded that the churches have a right to enter political debates, but they have special responsibilities 'to the facts, to their congregations and to their faiths'. But, he claimed, church leaders are looking for 'cheap headlines', they hog the limelight on complex political issues, they indulge in 'partisan politicking', have moved away from 'core beliefs' toward relativism, 'lost sight of the fundamentals' and filled the vacuum with politically correct causes like the environment, feminism, gay agendas, indigenous rights and indulged in 'ecclesiastical post-modernism'. Giving an example of a core belief he mentioned the resurrection, a clear reference to Carnley who had written a particularly thoughtful book, *The Structure of Resurrection Belief*.[42] Downer was particularly annoyed about criticism of the Iraq invasion; this, of course, was at a time when 'weapons of mass destruction' were still believed to exist by Downer and others. His advice for church leaders was that they should 'forego the opportunity to be amateur commentators on all manner of secular issues on which they inevitably lack expertise, and instead to find the spark of inspiration to give our lives greater moral and spiritual meaning'. Of course, the same could be applied to Downer himself.

What does all this tell you? Basically that the churches, especially the Catholic church, are still very much part of the Australian mainstream, although this is not often recognised. The media particularly tend to focus on the so-called 'mega-churches' like Hillsong as though they had replaced the traditional mainstream religious communities. Journalists are deceived by the apparent massive crowds, the movement, contemporary music and modern appearance. But much of this is superficial. The traditional churches are comparatively empty, their congregations aged. But this is a deceptive picture because their roots have sunk deep within Australian society and, as we saw, the range of services they provide is extensive.

But being a mainstream church, however, brings both strengths and weaknesses. Perhaps the primary strength is that Catholicism can communicate with and influence society because it is a genuine participant. But perhaps the biggest weakness is that 'arrival' is usually accompanied by pressure to conform. Catholics could lose their prophetic, critical edge, failing to emphasise the 'hard' words of Jesus, the challenge to 'the world', as Saint John's gospel says. In the New Testament the word 'world' is taken in theological rather than a cosmological sense: 'For what will it profit them [Jesus' followers] to gain the whole world and forfeit their life?'(Mark 8:36). For Saint Paul there is a constant struggle between the spirit of this world and the spirit of God. In the Letter to the Galatians Paul prays that 'I never boast of anything except the cross of Our Lord Jesus Christ by which the world has been crucified to me and I to the world' (6:14). Benedict XVI has emphasised the need for the recovery of a sense of Catholic identity, particularly in the face of militant Islam and the post-modern tendency to exclude religion entirely from public life. But he certainly doesn't envisage a retreat to a Catholic ghetto.[43]

One of the public areas where Australian Catholicism has failed significantly is in its relationship to the media. Usually the church blames the media for this and, on the occasions when Catholicism crosses their consciousness, the media blames the church for refusing to communicate. Regularly secular journalists come to me for comment as a 'last resort' when official Catholic commentators have refused to make any statement, sometimes on the most innocuous issues. The situation has been exacerbated by the sexual abuse crisis; the church's reputation has been badly tarnished by this issue. It is true that the majority of journalists reflect the secular, small 'l' liberal view of the world and are not particularly church-friendly, nor are they well informed about Catholicism specifically and religion generally, and they are often influenced by ecclesiastical stereotypes and caricatures. Outside the Religious Department of the ABC which employs a small pool of specialists, there are only about four or five other well-informed religious journalists working for Australia's daily newspapers. Over the last 20 years I have been intimately involved in the interface between church and media and this has given me a chance to reflect on what has often been a strained and difficult relationship.

A major part of the problem is that both parties harbour ill-informed stereotypes of each other. The church sees the media in oppositional terms: churchmen and official Catholics are often convinced that journalists are out to 'get' them and that, with a few exceptions, both print and electronic media are dominated by secularists and anti-Catholics who are determined to present the church badly and are always looking for faults and failures which are constantly highlighted, often unfairly. The feeling is that the media never covers Catholicism's strengths and successes; they are buried in a morass of bad publicity. In a recent Pastoral Letter on the media Australia's Catholic bishops complained that 'the church has suffered at the hands of the media ... Often the church is singled out for criticism because its message is profoundly and radically counter-cultural in this secular age.'[44]

While there is a grain of truth in this claim, the reasons for the criticism are much simpler. The media and journalists, when they do think about the church – which is not very often – are more or less convinced that Catholicism is a secretive, centrally-controlled, hierarchical organisation that is not responsible to anyone except the pope and hierarchy. The bishops' own behaviour in the sexual abuse crisis encouraged this attitude, and there is a feeling abroad that at its worst the church has sheltered pedophiles and sees itself above the law. At best the church is seen as a kind of 'colour piece'; a human interest story of no great significance.

The recent jettisoning of limbo is a case in point. In the Middle Ages the concept of limbo came about as a response to Augustine's opinion that because of the absolute necessity of baptism, unbaptised infants or virtuous unbelievers would go to hell. As I recently discovered this is a very hard thing to explain live on-air. My presenter was determined to turn the whole thing into a joke; he seemed befuddled and didn't know what else to do. Not knowing Catholicism's intellectual tradition, many journalists see the church as essentially fundamentalist; they see the discussion of odd things like limbo as a waste of time. These are unconscious, unarticulated stereotypes and not everybody holds them in their entirety, but they do act as caricatures that impregnate the whole interaction. On both sides there is mutual ignorance: rarely has one side any clue as to how the other works.

The Age religion reporter, Barney Zwartz, has pointed out the difficulties that the informed religion reporter faces. 'There are hardly any religion specialists in the media in Australia, there is no instructor, and it's a subject that often inspires strong passions.' He outlines the essence of the task: 'I have to satisfy the editors not that a story is worthy, but that it is newsworthy, a much harder task. I have to present it powerfully, bring out the controversial aspects, so that people will understand why it is important. I have to be fair, accurate and balanced, and provide context.' He also points out the reporter has to deal with religious communities under siege, like Australian Muslims.[45] Also many in the media are fixated on particular stories which are covered relentlessly. 'When I took the job, there were three main religion stories,' Zwartz says. 'One, the church is dying. Two, the troglodyte church gets in the way of gays and women. Three, priests and pedophilia. All of these are important, but if that's all you ever write about you're missing the story.'[46]

More deeply entrenched than the stereotype is the media's assumption that the church has nothing significant to say on the issues that trouble people today. Geraldine Doogue has pointed out that the *Australian Financial Review* annually gathers 25 'interested observers to assess who are really powerful in

Australian public life, those who affect the course of debate and set their own agenda'. She observed that 'not one mentioned the churches, which is an interesting benchmark about attitudes'.[47] Doogue suggests that part of the problem is that the media usually seeks out specialists in an age of focused expertise, but that they also value generalists, people like Hugh Mackay who tend to have broad knowledge and are highly articulate. But why aren't religious people at least called on to talk about questions of meaning, ethics and spirituality? Partly for the reasons stated above, but also because, as Doogue says, 'those who are used as sages, as providers of genuine help and clarity where people need it in terms of making sense of their lives, are usually the psychologists, writers and artists ... [They] use language that really can unlock deep and profound road-blocks in contemporary mind-sets and satisfy searchers for ways ahead.' She refers specifically to people like novelist David Malouf, American psychologist Martin Seligman, and interfaith minister, Stephanie Dowrick. Doogue correctly points out that in many ways these people are actually drawing on 'a profound reservoir of thoughts which do draw on the great Christian tradition'. Doogue's judgment is that the contemporary world 'is not a value-free, conscience-free zone at all. Quite the reverse. There is a plethora of searching, overtly and covertly underway, with quite elaborate and imaginative forums being devised.' I would also point out that in Australia there is a strongly-secular 'gate-keeping' class that either consciously or not firmly maintain control of who has media access and who doesn't. These are the people who make sure that they are consulted by the electronic media and are always the first to have an opinion piece ready for the print media.

One reason why the church is often left out of discussion is because Catholic representatives still seem to have difficulty with public discourse, although those who can handle the media are often consulted, people like Jesuit priest, Father Frank Brennan and Catholic Health Australia's, Francis Sullivan. But bishops and official Catholics seem to find it hard to understand that in a pluralist-democratic society we work our way toward agreed moral, ethical and societal standards and values by way of public discourse in which the media plays an essential part. This is why talk-back radio is so pervasive. People love to hear what others think about all types of things from moral standards and social mores to good manners and correct behaviour. We debate our standards; they are not handed down from above as absolutes. Off-the-shelf answers and authoritative pronouncements are no longer believed. This is very hard for the hierarchical mind-set to comprehend. That is why some bishops find it difficult to engage in broad, wide-ranging discussions which are based on the principle that every point of view has a right to be considered. It is hard to do this if you think that you already have the truth.

As we have seen the Australian church still has a vast ministerial structure which, while it may sometimes bog Catholics down in institutions, is still a foundation on which to build. People today are much more receptive and open to faith than they were in the late '80s and early '90s. The renewed interest in spirituality, ethics and finding a meaning structure to guide our lives gives the church an opportunity, a chance to speak again of the teaching of Jesus and the gospels. I certainly don't share the kind of narrow pessimism reflected in Michael Gilchrist's *Lost! Australia's Catholics Today* (2006). He blames 'the papal critics' who, he says are today's 'real reactionaries … trapped as they are in their 60s and 70s time warp and spiritual blinkers'.[48] Sure, those of us of the Vatican II generation have made serious mistakes and errors of judgment, but the decades after Vatican II were complex and Catholics like Gilchrist offer only simplistic solutions to the complex historical process through which the church and our society is passing.

In the next chapter I want to try to delineate some of the key issues that I think Australian Catholicism is facing, and move on to look at some of the possible solutions.

3

Catholics adrift

Despite all of the positive things happening in the church, Australian Catholics are still 'a people adrift'.[1] Many feel that the church is bereft of leadership and lacks direction. Certainly the Australian Catholic Bishops' Conference (ACBC) has shown some leadership in some areas, but people feel that there is a failure to follow through, often because the bishops are looking over their shoulders to Rome. It's also true that many of the laity who were once very committed have withdrawn, and a sizeable proportion feel that the 'official' church has abandoned them because it is uninterested in their concerns. A doctor friend of mine, with years of experience in family medicine said to me: 'I don't feel as though I left the church; I feel the church left me!' What he means is the church is not addressing or even comprehending the questions that Catholics face in contemporary life. For most, these questions focus on the credibility of belief, gender, pluralism, equality, institutional corruption and at the deepest level, spirituality. Many feel that church leaders don't appreciate what it is like to survive economically and bring up a family in modern Australia.

This sense of alienation is particularly true of women. This is made abundantly clear in *Woman and Man. One in Christ Jesus*, a comprehensive report on the participation of women in the Australian Catholic church commissioned in August 1996 by the ACBC.[2] The process involved the largest research and consultation project ever undertaken by the Australian Catholic church. If nothing else, it indicated that there was a realisation among some of the bishops that something had to be done about the relationship between women and Catholicism. It involved a series of hearings held in capital cities and provincial centres with every diocese participating. It aimed to gather data on the participation of women in the Catholic church to 'provide a solid basis for theological reflection, pastoral planning and dialogue with women and women's groups'. The response was extraordinary, showing clearly that women's participation is a key issue for the future of Catholicism.

> The dominant issue arising from the research was gender equality ...
> The Church seemed to be lagging behind the wider Australian society in recognising the changing role of women ... and affirming the equality of women.

There was a call for women to participate 'in decision-making at all levels' and the promotion of 'opportunities for women to participate in leadership in the church'. While the Report pointed out that women contributed enormously to the work of the church, it was usually in 'ancillary and support roles' and they were largely excluded from 'the ordained ministry, leadership and decision-making'. The Report was unequivocal that 'There was much agreement, even among those with different views on the question, that there should be open discussion of the issue of women's ordination.'[3]

I still vividly remember the day in August 1999 at the National Press Club in Canberra when the co-ordinator of the project, Dr Marie Macdonald (the first Australian woman to become a Doctor of Theology), presented the Report. She told the assembled media, bishops and interested parties that during their hearings around Australia she and her colleagues found

> a strong sense of pain and alienation resulting from the Church's stance on women. A dichotomous relationship with the Church, characterised by such feelings as love and commitment yet anguish and alienation, was experienced by both individuals and groups. Pain, alienation and often anger resulted from a strong sense of women's marginalisation ... and lack of acknowledgment within the Church.

She spoke of people's feelings of frustration as they tried to remain within the church, and of the sadness of those who felt they had to leave over this issue. 'It was clear', she said, 'that many people have hope but in many cases it is faint'.

The real feel of what is happening 'out there' came from the testimony of women quoted in the Report. A woman in Hobart, for instance, said that she

> was offended by the suggestion that as a woman I am 'inappropriate' for certain ministries within the church. I make decisions with people about their lives every day, and I am offended to be excluded from making decisions within the church because I am a woman. I personally do not want to be a priest, but I do not want to be barred from full participation in the Catholic church because of a combination of chromosomes that made me a woman.[4]

The Report commented that at the hearings

> the presentations were mainly from people who are still committed to the Church. A strong sense of deep faith and love and commitment to the church were evident. However, love and tolerance of others were not always shown. Some had trouble hearing a viewpoint different from a conservative stance and obedience ranked higher than charity.

The Report noted the sheer diversity of views and recorded that 'much emphasis was placed on the value of pluralism, unity and diversity, and the need to strive for wholeness and inclusivity'.[5]

The bishops responded a year later. Essentially they committed themselves to develop a 'better balance' of men and women, clergy and laity, on national episcopal bodies, to foster research on the participation of women in ministry and the life of the church, to 'drawing up guidelines concerning the use of inclusive language in the liturgy, prayer, pastoral and social life of the church', and to 'respond to the pain of people and groups within the church who are struggling with the implications of church teaching' regarding divorce and remarriage, the exclusion of women from ordination, sexuality, marriage and family planning. They also committed to establishing a Council for Australian Catholic Women (CACW).

It all sounded positive at the time, but eight years later progress has been snail-pace slow. The CACW has been set up and executive officers appointed. From CACW's reports to the bishops it is clear that they have attempted to make contact with a wide range of organisations in the church and build bridges with dioceses and parishes. They have focused on the participation of young women in the life of the church and have set up a 10-week fellowship, through which women can receive the theological and professional training to engage in interfaith relationships. This began in 2005. They have also tried to deal with the question of inclusive language in worship, but without success. The stumbling block here has been the refusal of the Vatican Congregation for Divine Worship and the International Commission on English in the Liturgy to consider the issue of inclusive language.

One area where women could be involved at a leadership level is in diocesan administrations. A check of the 2007–08 Catholic Directory shows that the results are mixed. Quite a number of dioceses have employed laypeople in senior positions and most Australian bishops have a woman secretary or executive officer. The size of diocesan curiae (or administrations) vary from small in places like Cairns and Bunbury to large in Melbourne, Brisbane and Sydney. Laywomen and laymen are employed in almost equal numbers (about 150 women and 160 men) in curiae and they vary as to how many women they have in senior positions. Generally there are more senior men than women, although some middle-sized dioceses such as Adelaide, Canberra–Goulburn, Hobart, Parramatta, Perth and Wollongong score very well on women in senior positions, as do some smaller dioceses such as Broome, Geraldton, Rockhampton, Toowoomba and Townsville. Large dioceses like Melbourne and Brisbane, in contrast, have very few women in senior positions. However, the Australian church is far ahead of the Vatican. There are only two women in senior positions in the Roman Curia. The secretary of state, Cardinal Tarcisio Bertone, suggested in early July 2007 that more women be employed in the Vatican, but at the time of writing no practical steps had been taken to implement this.[6]

Benedict XVI also has two vowed laywomen on his personal staff, Birgit Wansing whom he brought with him from the Congregation for the Doctrine of the Faith (CDF), and musician Ingrid Stampa, a viola da gamba player and former professor at Hamburg's Musikhochschule.

These women are not housekeepers, but trusted assistants and advisors. In the Vatican pecking order Stampa ranks alongside Monsignor Georg Gänswein, the Pope's priest secretary. She has kept a low profile but Vatican insiders are convinced that she has a real influence on the German Pope. These are minuscule practical steps for women, even if Benedict has made it clear that, in theory at least, he believes women played an important role in the life of Jesus and in the early Christian church.[7] When questioned about his attitudes to women he said that 'our faith and the constitution of the college of the Apostles obliges us and doesn't allow us to confer priestly ordination on women'.[8] However, he added 'I believe that women themselves with their energy and strength, with their superiority, with what I'd call their "spiritual power" will know how to make their own space.' He promised 'to try and listen to God so as not to stand in their way'. It is not clear what he meant by 'making their own space'; some took it to mean that he was not entirely closed to ordination of women although that is hard to square with what he said previously. Perhaps he was simply trying to indicate that the question of the role of women was not closed. But while not sounding quite as patronising as his predecessor, John Paul II, it is clear that nothing is going to change in this papacy to actualise what Benedict calls women's 'spiritual power'. That power will only be released when women have access to all the ministries of the church.

In the years since the Report was published the Australian church has done very little and the alienation of women, especially younger women, grows deeper, even though 76 per cent of pastoral care in the Australian church is carried out by women. One of the most striking findings of *Woman and Man* was that women comprised 74 per cent of those undertaking undergraduate studies in theology and almost 64 per cent of post-graduate theological students. Thus the church already has a highly trained cadre of women to take part in the ministry and the priesthood as soon as that becomes a possibility. This is (as one woman put it in the Sydney hearings) 'an enormous potential resource for the Church'.[9]

But this talent is being neglected. The hierarchy is completely hamstrung by the Vatican's ineffective prohibition on talking about women's ordination and ministry. The movement for the Ordination of Catholic Women (OCW) has taken one of the most creative approaches to this issue. In its most recent pamphlet 'Duty Bound to Lead' OCW calls for a renewed priestly ministry. It says that

> [a] renewed ordained ministry of both women and men [will] function in
> a relational rather than hierarchical manner ... Our desire is to operate
> in a faith community that nurtures values of equality, inclusiveness,
> understanding and tolerance, one which encourages a transcendent
> spirituality that is imbued with a sense of compassion and the ability to
> reach beyond oneself ... We believe a renewed ordained ministry with
> women and men having an equal role in leading the church is integral
> to sustaining the precious gift of the Catholic faith that has formed us. A
> renewed ordained ministry would revitalise pastoral care and sacramental
> ministry.[10]

The pamphlet sets out a theological foundation for this renewed approach to ministry; it is underpinned by a pervasive concern about passing on the faith to future generations. I have often been struck by the lack of passion for communicating the faith to younger people among Catholics, some of them priests or religious people. There is a kind of tired, defeatist attitude that somehow the future will look after itself, or that 'God will provide', or nothing can be done. OCW, on the other hand, is deeply concerned about communicating the faith to the coming generation. Perhaps this is because most are parents and mothers and they have a feel for the task of nurturing faith in the next generation. They are also aware of how alienated their daughters are from a church that doesn't treat women as equals.

The need for the renewal of priestly ministry and the question of the ordination of women cannot be side-stepped, no matter how often the hierarchy attempt to wash their hands of this issue. A decisive shift has occurred within the church. The papal teaching about the exclusion of women from the ordained ministry has not been received by the faithful, just like the teaching on contraception. Church teaching must be authenticated by the Catholic community. The church must eventually accept what is proposed. If a teaching has not been received by the faithful over a reasonable period of time, then it can be argued that it is not the teaching of the church. This is certainly the case regarding the prohibition of contraception, and I believe it can also be reasonably applied to the question of the ordination of women.

The call for the renewal of priestly ministry leads straight into the next topic: priests.

Nowadays priests seem to be the focus of every controversy in the church. The priesthood has become a lightning rod for issues like the role of the laity, clericalism, the exclusion of women from ordained ministry, celibacy, reproductive ethics, sexual identity, access to the sacraments and Mass, even the relevance and meaning of Catholicism itself. This is because the priest sits at the crossroads between the hierarchy and laity and is the most readily accessible ecclesiastical figure. He lives locally and answers his own phone. Since Vatican II the role of the priest has been in flux. Many mature and experienced priests are spiritually closer to the laity than the hierarchy because they have adopted a collaborative model of ministry. Of course there are still a lot of parishes where 'Father' reigns supreme and where the domination of the clergy and subordination of the laity is seen as a matter of 'divine law'. In fact a sizeable number of people report that it was conflict with a priest that led them to leave the church.[11]

On the other hand some priests consider that they are blamed unfairly for every problem in the church and feel that they are under siege as they struggle to meet the pastoral needs of their parishes. This starts with their workload, but it is complicated by the fact that they live on the job, which makes them easily accessible. Some are motivated by messianic pretensions that they have to respond to every request and demand. This is compounded by the fact that they are aging. Also, as I myself found, the institution has a way of 'grabbing' you. Priorities such as finance, building maintenance, administration and a host of immediate problems can drown you in detail. Many parishes are, in fact, quite sizeable small businesses with a reasonably high turnover; one can easily become trapped in priorities that are not ministerial. Some of this can be turned over to laypeople, but the way parishes are presently structured means that the priest has to take ultimate responsibility for the viability of the whole operation. I personally found that there was nothing worse than having to ask for money.

I also found that I experienced many frustrations engendered by conflicts between my own ministerial instincts and experience on the one hand, and church law on the other. A couple of issues tend to focus these frictions. One of the most common is marriage. Nowadays 76 per cent of all couples presenting for marriage are cohabiting. Couples can be sheepish and embarrassed when they approach a priest, often projecting onto him their unconscious feelings of guilt. Most have little sense of the meaning of marriage as a sacrament and are sometimes resistant to preparation programs, most of which these days are soundly psychologically based. Some who would prefer to marry in a secular context only come to the priest because they are responding to family pressures. Many people want to design their own marriage service and celebrate it outside a church building in a place that is meaningful to them. Most dioceses will not allow this and pastorally-sensitive priests get caught in the middle. As a result couples are abandoning the church and turning to civil celebrants. In 2005 'marriages performed by civil celebrants ... outnumbered marriages performed by ministers of religion. This trend commenced in 1999 when 51 per cent of marriages were performed by civil celebrants. By 2005 this proportion had increased to 60 per cent.'[12] There is no sign of this trend changing. Catholic priests, however, are still the most regular religious celebrants with a third of all church marriages.

The priest's ministerial frustrations don't cease with the ceremony. Divorce has become another hurdle to be negotiated. In 2005 52 399 divorces were granted in Australia, which is a slight decrease from the record high of 2001 when 55 330 were granted. To get some idea of the statistical meaning of this there were 13.1 divorces per 1000 married people in 2001. The 2005 median age for divorce was 42.1 years and the median duration from marriage to separation was 8.8 years.[13] Divorced people, of course, can receive Communion, but what happens when they enter into a new relationship? Unless they have obtained a church annulment, they are excluded from a second marriage in the church and from Communion. Yet this is often precisely the time when people most need spiritual and sacramental support. Over the last couple of decades many priests recommended what was called an 'internal forum' solution; after discussion with a sympathetic priest divorced Catholics who remarried outside the church made a judgment of conscience that they were not barred from Communion. However, in mid-September 1994 the then-Cardinal Joseph Ratzinger intervened with a letter to all bishops in which he excluded this pastoral solution. He said that 'the Church affirms that a new union cannot be recognised as valid if the preceding marriage was valid. If the divorced are remarried civilly … they cannot receive Holy Communion as long as this situation persists.'[14]

A decade later, the now-Pope Ratzinger was more compassionate. In the same discussion in which he referred to Australia as 'Godless', he referred to the 'painful situation' of those who in their youth were 'not really believers' and who married in the church 'just for tradition', then divorced and remarried. They then convert or recover their faith but they are now excluded from Communion. Saying that 'None of us has a ready-made solution because each person's situation is different', he didn't really offer any practical solution to this problem beyond insisting on welcoming them to the parish and saying when he was CDF Prefect he consulted the bishops and that they told him they found the problem 'very difficult'.[15] Local priests, however, can't get off the hook quite so easily as bishops and popes. They have to deal face to face with good, sincere people who genuinely want to go to Communion. It is the local priest, not the pope or the bishop, who is expected to go against his experience and ministerial instincts to tell them they can't approach Communion.

Fortunately most priests have more sense and advise people that even the Cardinal Prefect of the CDF is not infallible and cannot contradict personal conscience, for in the end it is conscience which must ultimately guide people. But none of this is easy for priests.

The most crippling reality that priests have to face is the sexual abuse crisis. They find themselves the butt of nasty jokes, their profession derided and they are looked upon with considerable suspicion by people who often know nothing about the Catholic church and certainly don't know any priests personally. In the Boston archdiocese (which has been the storm-centre of the sexual abuse crisis in the US), many priests were said to be suffering from post-traumatic stress-like symptoms. Compounding the situation is a trend by people including victims, their champions, elements of the media, and some lawyers, to get revenge on the church, and particularly on priests.[16] Understandably priests feel that they are vulnerable targets. If they are accused they know they will be stood down and have little hope of ever recovering their reputation.

No one is denying that sexual abuse of children is horrendous and intolerable and that the failure of the church to deal with it effectively has done immeasurable damage to victims. The cover-ups, the protection of abusive clergy and the refusal to admit egregious mistakes are unjustifiable. I still remember my friend, the late Father Robert Bullock, a senior parish priest in the Boston archdiocese and one of the leaders of the Boston priests whose protests led to the removal of Cardinal Bernard Law as archbishop, saying that we have not yet even begun to calculate the damage these crimes have done to people's trust and to the reputation of the church. Law had simply moved demonstrably abusive priests from parish to parish, thus giving them access to new victims. While some indications in the US may suggest that the negative impact is short-term and the worst is over, I suspect that Bullock was right. There is no doubt that the clerical profession has taken a severe battering and that respect for the priesthood is, understandably, at an all-time low. Young people – and their elders – are rightly sceptical about everything the church says about gender and sexuality. But this has a flow-on effect with the church's entire message, especially its challenging social justice message and cultural critique, equally dismissed. Trust is going to have to be built from the bottom up by bishops and priests before their pronouncements on morality will be taken seriously again, so perhaps it would be best of they took a vow of silence about these issues for several decades to come!

Nowadays, however, ecclesiastical superiors are proactive and move with alacrity when accusations are made. Some priests now feel authorities have moved too far towards the other end of the spectrum. This feeling has been re-enforced by the experience that accused priests have had of the church's own processes. In what must be a first, the progressive-leaning National Council of Priests (NCP) joined with the more clerically-oriented Australian Con-fraternity of Catholic Clergy to review the experience of priests in dealing with accusations of abuse.[17] This process is set out in the document 'Towards Healing' (2000) which outlines principles and procedures for dealing with allegations against clergy.[18] The review also looked at diocesan Professional Standards Offices as well the therapeutic program, 'Encompass Australasia' set up by the ACBC and religious orders to deal with the psychological and sexual problems of clergy and members of religious orders.

The review found that the rights of accused priests are often 'overlooked or ignored', that they had often not been given legal advice or experienced support persons. They were frequently cajoled into making admissions and agreeing to resign, or were sent to Encompass assessments and programs under pressure. Priests are assumed to be guilty, their rights to fairness and a presumption of innocence ignored, and they are dismissed from ministry by bishops or superiors without any legal process, often before they have been afforded the opportunity to defend themselves. Accused priests have been kept in the dark by bishops withholding accusations or aspects of accusa-tions. There is confusion between what are actually 'boundary violations', that is consensual adult sexual encounters, and the sexual abuse of children, which falls under the jurisdictions of criminal and canon law. Priests accused of consensual adult sex are treated as if they were child abusers. Particular criticism is levelled at Encompass. The review asked whether Encompass tries 'to help the priest who may be ill, psychologically or otherwise, or to help the priest's bishop find a way of dealing with him. It is our experience that Encompass … personnel have encouraged and even cajoled depressed and medicated priests to disclose internal forum matters to the bishop.' The review also commented that in the rush to protect the institution's reputation and the bishop's hide, the legal rights of priests to a fair process and the presumption of innocence were ignored. A similar situation has emerged in the UK where a church lawyer who defends accused priests said that 'bishops cannot be trusted to help priests accused of child abuse'.[19]

In this kind of atmosphere it is understandable that the majority of good priests nowadays are careful about lifting their heads above the ruck. Most have withdrawn to their own parishes where they feel they can achieve something in co-operation with laypeople who know and trust them. As one priest put it 'A parish is a bit like a franchise operation. As long as you hang out the right signage you can pretty much do what you like.' There are a few free spirits like Father Bob Maguire from Saint Peter and Paul Parish in South Melbourne who defied convention by appearing with John Safran on SBS TV in the shows *John Safran Versus God* and *Speaking in Tongues,* as well as being a frequent guest on commercial radio and TV shows. His down-to-earth way of speaking and self-depreciating humour make him an ideal media performer. Jesuit Father Frank Brennan is widely respected – even if Paul Keating called him a 'meddlesome priest' – because he has fearlessly articulated the church's social teaching, represented the church in some of the hardest questions that cross the political-religious divide, defended Aborigines and refugees, and written a book on conscience in public life, that is widely read and respected.[20] But few other priests speak out, although a number in Sydney, such as Father John Crothers, have been fearlessly critical of archdiocesan pastoral policy, and Father Eric Hodgens in Melbourne has criticised Catholic Education Office (CEO) policy and has crunched the statistics showing the acute shortage of priests in Australia.

The shortage of priests takes us to the heart of the internal problems facing the Australian church. For its entire history Catholicism has always been a liturgical, worshiping community with the celebration of baptism, Eucharist and the sacraments at the centre of its life. The core ministry of the priest is to provide these celebrations. Because worship is so integral to the essence of Catholicism, it is logical to conclude that a church leadership that fails, no matter what the reason, to provide local communities with reasonable access to liturgy and above all to the Mass, introduces a distortion, even a heresy into the heart of Catholic life. When the reason is the requirement of celibacy as a precondition for ordination, at most a third or fourth level issue in the pantheon of Catholicism, this imposition must be challenged. It is vividly illustrated in Latin America: on average there is one priest to every 15 000 Catholics. 'Apart from being very few in number, the priests are poorly educated. Concubinage is a common practise in the rural areas and in the Andes. In many churches and parishes Sunday Mass is celebrated rarely.'[21]

The simple reality is that in many parts of the world Catholicism is facing a sacramental and ministerial crisis due to the catastrophic drop in the number of priests and in those presenting for training to the priesthood. While this is not true of every country, it is certainly true of the developed Western world, including Australia, and many parts of the developing world. The local situation is highlighted by the statistical work of Father Eric Hodgens.[22] But the priest shortage is not a new issue; many have been warning about it since the mid-1970s. But there was an absolute refusal by John Paul II, the Vatican and most bishops to confront the issue. What the Vatican has done is to try to force local bishops to set-up stopgap measures, such as Sunday Worship in Absence of a Priest (SWAP). In a catastrophic situation they were still vaguely praying for an increase in 'vocations'. Maintaining clerical celibacy and the present style of ministry is judged more important than providing local communities with the Mass and sacraments.

The obligation to justify their approach lies on those who demand lifelong commitment to celibacy before ordination when, as a result, Mass and the sacraments become unavailable to large numbers of Catholics. These people are the real non-traditional revolutionaries. By demanding celibacy they create an artificial shortage of priests, which limits access to the liturgy. They are the ones changing the essential nature of the church. The genuine traditionalists are those calling for a renewed priestly ministry that jettisons the absolute obligation of celibacy and places the celebration of Mass and the sacraments as the top priority, as it always has been throughout the history of Catholicism. Edward Schillebeeckx has argued strongly that criteria for admission to the ordained ministry can never gainsay the apostolic right to sacramental ministry.[23] The Mass is far more important than a lifestyle requirement like celibacy.

Let's call a spade a spade: from a theological perspective there is a distinct danger that in order to protect the link between celibacy and ordination, recent popes have been engaged, whether they recognise it or not, in distorting an essential element of Catholic belief. To do that is to move in the direction of heresy. The person most responsible here is John Paul II; his long papacy blocked ministry questions from being considered at an official level, despite the efforts of millions of Catholics hungering for the Mass and the sacraments. A number of courageous bishops, such as the Indonesian Bishops' Conference, challenged him on the pastoral crisis; but he did not listen. Benedict XVI has shown no leadership on this issue either. In mid-November 2006 he re-affirmed celibacy as a requirement for ordination in the Western church. There is no indication that anything will be done about the shortage of priests in this papacy, except to paper-over the problem. So now we face a disaster.

Church history provides a context here. The law was universally imposed on the Western church in the second half of the 11th and the first part of the 12th centuries. Even the apostles were married and all three synoptic gospels speak of Saint Peter's mother-in-law, so the first pope must have had a wife (Matthew 8:14–15; Mark 1:30–31; Luke 4:38–39). During the first millennium the vast majority of clergy and bishops were married, as were many of the popes and, despite the attempts of some reformist local councils to impose celibacy, clerical marriage was the recognised norm. It has never been universally imposed in the eastern Orthodox church and there are a number of eastern-rite Catholic churches in union with Rome which have always had married priests.

What we have inherited from the medieval world is the clerical system, the notion that priests are somehow sacred, separate from and superior to 'ordinary' Catholics. Already many Australian priests especially from the older, Vatican II generation have broken out of this attitude and have substantially thrown in their lot with the laity.[24] In fact it is the more mature priests who have done most to strip themselves of privilege and power and to care for and nurture the gifts of others. These are some of the most generous and ministerial of men. Over the last few decades hardly anyone uses the title 'Father'. Most priests and even bishops are addressed by their baptismal name. A further symbol of this is that very few Australian priests wear clerical dress; this is true even among the more conservative clergy. The only worrying sign here is the revived clericalism of some younger clergy and seminary students.

Jane Anderson's Australian research in her book *Priests in Love* shows the real issue regarding celibacy is not sexuality, but power. The celibate priest is the church's man, tied to the institution through a whole system of intimate interconnections, spiritual, social, economic and professional. As one of her priest confidants told her: 'The whole issue is *not* about celibacy, ordination of women, married priests, etc, etc. It is about authority, leadership and power. As it has been from day one.'[25] This is illustrated by the fact that the way things operate in Australia means that the priest has little or no life of his own. He is financially and domestically tied to the church through low wages and modest, but usually comfortable, domestic arrangements which double as his place of work. Most priests are paid between $1000 to $1200 per month depending on the diocese and their seniority. Urban priests tend to be better paid than those in rural dioceses. They are also provided with a car through various schemes, some more generous than others.

But, as Anderson says, the paradigm in which priests work is literally often 'lethal' to them. They are on duty 24 hours a day, live on the job in the presbytery, and have to assume 'high levels of responsibility for the lives of others'. They have to be jacks-of-all-trades and 'the sacralisation of the priesthood also evokes an idealisation of the clergy by the laity, placing huge expectations on priests'. The result is burn-out and extremely high levels of stress. As

Anderson shows this occasionally results in the tragedy of priestly suicide.[26] Because of the lack of separation of their personal and professional lives this can also result in the loss of personal boundaries and the occurrence of what clerical professional standards organisations call 'boundary violations'. No matter what the circumstances, it is always the priest who is blamed when this occurs. No one ever considers the conditions under which priests often have to live and of the expectations that are projected onto them. It is the great strength of Anderson's book that she considers these factors and the personal impact of all of this on the individual priest. Her research is unique and original, probably the first time it has even been done.

Despite repeated, but unsubstantiated claims by many in ecclesiastical authority that the numerical collapse has bottomed-out and that increasing numbers of priestly vocations are coming to the seminary, it is clear that no such bottoming-out has occurred. With continued resignations from active ministry, a high average age, retirement and an increasing death-rate, Australian Catholicism is well below the basic priest-replacement rate, despite the fact that there is an escalation in the number of Catholics.

But rather than assisting already overworked priests and providing for the worship of the vast majority of Catholics, Benedict XVI has focused on a tiny, totally unrepresentative group of Catholics; those who demand the restoration of the Latin Mass. In his decree *Summorum Pontificium* (7 July 2007) the Pope asked priests to provide special Masses in Latin according to the pre-Vatican II, 16th century Tridentine liturgy, which established the form of the Mass and sacraments prior to Vatican II. Attendance at Latin Masses in Australia is minuscule. The secretary of the National Liturgical Council, Father Peter Williams, estimates that of the three-quarters of a million people attending Mass on any given Sunday in Australia no more that 1400 to 1800 attend Latin Masses.[27] These people are already served by eight priests from the Priestly Fraternity of Saint Peter celebrating Latin Masses in Sydney, Melbourne and Canberra. At that rate there is one priest to every 225 Latin Mass-attendees.

But this concession to a tiny minority has a deeper relevance. As several senior French bishops, including Cardinal Jean-Pierre Ricard of Bordeaux and Cardinal André Vingt-Trois of Paris pointed out, support for the pre-Vatican II Mass is a covert symbol of a deeper refusal to accept the theology and reforms of Vatican II. 'The traditionalists consider the Latin Mass as the flag of a wider cause', Cardinal Ricard said, 'since a religious rite is more than a liturgical expression, it is a political vision of the Church and the world.'[28] No matter what Benedict might claim, this concession is essentially about a roll-back of the liturgical and pastoral reform of Vatican II; because liturgical prayer is at the heart of what it means to be a Catholic, and touches on a whole range of other issues. The liturgical scholar, Rita Ferrone, points out that the theological emphases embedded in the pre-Vatican II liturgy shifts the emphasis away from Christ's resurrection back to the expiation of sin, it limits the use of Scripture, and excludes the community and particularly women from participation. It is anti-ecumenical and indicates the influence of a small group with considerable influence in the Vatican Congregation for Worship who call for 'a reform of the reform'; in other words, a rolling back of Vatican II.[29]

But back to the mainstream: the median age of Australian priests is 61. Most are over-committed, working almost seven days a week with hardly any time off. Burn-out and mental and physical exhaustion are common. Recruitment is down to an all-time-low. For instance, the Melbourne seminary which serves 1 350 000 Catholics in Victoria and Tasmania has only recruited seven entrants per year for the last 15 years. 'To get the number of priests we need to match the present coverage we would need thirty a year', Hodgens says. Hodgens' work shows that 'the heyday for [priestly] recruitment was the mid-1950s. For every 100 000 Catholics 5.5 to 6.3 students [entered the seminary]. This was more than a 25 per cent increase on pre-war recruitment levels.' The retention rate of students – that is, how many went on to ordination – was between 33 per cent and 40 per cent at the start of the 1960s. Since the late-50s recruitment has steadily dropped. 'This continued for 35 years and settled in the mid-90s. The final rate was only 10 per cent of what it was at the peak.' Only about a third of those recruited proceed to ordination. At present the church is ordaining about 0.15 to 0.25 priests per 100 000 Catholics each year. There is no sign of an increase despite claims of slightly bigger numbers in the Sydney, Perth, Melbourne and Neo-Catechumenate seminaries.[30] Hodgens points out that the age of ordination has risen and that priests will have shorter periods of service. Until the mid-90s men were usually ordained around age 27 giving them about 38 years of service to the church. The average age of ordination is now 35, giving an average of 30 years of service. 'At this rate, even if they all stay priests, the long term result will be one priest for every 13 000 in Victoria and Queensland and one for every 22 000 in NSW.' In other words about 7.5 priests per 100 000 Catholics. Hodgens says 'That means that Melbourne with its one million plus Catholics and 220 parishes will have only 75 priests.'[31]

Historically, the average ratio of priests to people is the one represented in the pre-World War II period. For instance in the archdiocese of Melbourne the ratio of priests to people in 1887 was one to 2440 (if you exclude religious order priests) and one to 1800 (if they are included). Given that a minority of religious priests would be in parish ministry, the real figure is probably somewhere between these two, say one priest to every 2100 Catholics.[32] By 1947 the Catholic population had reached 255 000 and Melbourne had 234 diocesan priests and 220 religious priests. This gives a ratio of one to 561 (if all priests are counted) and one to 1089 (if only diocesan clergy are counted). The real figure again is probably about one priest to 750 Catholics.[33] Australia-wide in 1961 the Catholic population was 2.6 million and there were 2163 diocesan priests and 1191 religious priests working in Australia, a total of 3354.[34]

Figures for the United States are somewhat different to Australia. There the ratio of priests to people in 1900 was one priest to 900. In 1950 it was one to 650 and in 1999 one to 1200. But other variables need to be taken into account. The United States Conference of Catholic Bishops state:

> First, the age of priests in 1999 is much higher than it was in 1900. Second the … people … reflected much greater diversity than they did in 1900. Third, parish life is much more complex than it was 100 years ago [and a] whole new set of skills are required of today's pastors.[35]

These realities also apply in Australia.

The 2007–08 Catholic Directory lists 1996 diocesan priests and 1182 religious order priests serving 5.1 million Australian Catholics.[36] That is about one priest for every 1604 Catholics. However, a number of variables need to be taken into account. Probably less than half of religious order priests serve in parishes and the totals also sometimes include retired priests, priests otherwise assigned, or on-leave from the ministry. The real figure is probably one priest to about 2500 Catholics.[37] But this masks the real situation, because the superabundance of priests from the 1950s and 1960s are still moving through the system. These men are now close to, at, or beyond retirement age, with many of them still working hard just to keep parish structures going. Some priests have hung on into their 80s. But within a decade or less when the present generation retires or dies the crisis point will have been reached with no solution on the horizon. Hodgens comments that 'we will have a quarter of the number [of priests] we need in Victoria and Queensland and one-sixth in New South Wales'.

Hodgens' statistical analysis is backed up by experience on the ground. Take the archdiocese of Hobart, for instance, which covers the whole of Tasmania and the Bass Strait islands (an area equal to that of the Republic of Ireland). According to the 2007–08 Catholic Directory the archdiocese has 35 diocesan priests.[38] Only 17 of these are listed as working in parishes with the rest retired or on leave. There are also 15 religious priests working in parishes, although five of these serve at the inner-city Saint Joseph's in Hobart. The result is obvious: parishes have had to be combined, or pastoral associates, including six religious sisters and two laywomen, appointed. The Tasmanian crisis was highlighted in a 5 March 2006 ABC *Compass* program entitled 'A Parish with No Priest'.[39] The program focused on the north-east coast parish of Saint Marys that had just lost its priest: he died of a heart attack in his car driving between Masses in the parish which covered most of the east coast of Tasmania. Archbishop Adrian Doyle confessed to *Compass*:

Since I became archbishop [in 1999] there were eighteen priests who were active … who are no longer so. The majority of them have retired for health reasons, and there have been some deaths as well. I think it was the three deaths last year [2005] that seemed to accelerate the whole situation in a way that we probably hadn't expected or certainly hadn't planned for.

A young priest, Father Greg McGregor, aged 31, then on loan to Hobart from Sydney, put the problem succinctly:

A lot of our guys are in their fifties and sixties and in ten, fifteen years' time they'll be retiring. They've certainly earned it, they've worked so hard. And, I guess, as the big bubble kind of moves through to retirement and the next generation moves on, I'm really worried about what it's going to be like in the future.

Increasingly many of the smaller parishes in Tasmania have a SWAP led by a sister or layperson.

Another diocese that faces a priest shortage is Wilcannia–Forbes. It takes in the whole of the western division of New South Wales, stretching along the New South Wales–South Australian border from Queensland to Victoria. It is one and a half times the size of Italy and is divided into 20 parishes with a Catholic population of about 30 000 living either in towns or on farms and stations. But it only has 15 diocesan and three religious priests available for 20 parishes. The diocese of Townsville faces similar problems. The Townsville region has about 160 000 people of whom probably about 45 000 are Catholic. The diocese has 74 000 Catholics making up 29 per cent of the population. It includes the whole of central Queensland from the coast to the Northern Territory border, including Cloncurry and Mount Isa, and has 27 parishes. These are served by 15 diocesan priests and six religious priests; that is 21 priests for 27 parishes. A sister, four laywomen and one layman serve in parishes as either pastoral associates or parish leaders.[40]

At first glance the diocese of Toowoomba looks to be in good shape. It covers all of southern Queensland from just below the Great Dividing Range westward to the South Australian and Northern Territory borders, and is almost one-and-a-half times the size of Germany. It has 25 diocesan and three religious priests who cover 37 parishes. What is interesting about Toowoomba is that it has a Diocesan Pastoral Leadership Plan with a nine-year span that will conclude at Easter 2014. In his Advent Pastoral Letter of 2006 Bishop William Morris talked about the need for a 'deeper faith in God's Spirit at work in our time' and a genuine hope and mutual trust for the future.[41] He speaks about the need to work together 'with the human and material resources we have to hand … we accept the pastoral situation of our own day and work within it as people of faith and hope'. Based on present numbers and ages of priests Morris shows that in 2014 the diocese will be left with 14 priests aged between 61 and 70 working in parish-based ministry, and four priests between 65 and 70 working in diocesan ministry for the whole Toowoomba diocese with its 37 parishes. The situation could not be put more clearly and the reality is that this is the kind of situation that many dioceses will be facing in 2014. Bishop Morris also points out that there are other solutions 'for ensuring that the Eucharist may be celebrated' besides more SWAP celebrations. These are ordaining married men 'endorsed by their local parish community, welcoming former priests back to active ministry, ordaining women and recognising Anglican, Lutheran and Uniting church orders'.

This type of realism was not welcome in some quarters. No one knows who reported Morris to Rome, but within two months of the publication of the Advent Pastoral he was summonsed to the Vatican to explain himself. In response he pointed out that he was going to be in Rome for a conference in May anyway, and that he also had a priest dying and he wanted to remain in Toowoomba to support him. The next thing anyone knew was when an Apostolic Visitator was appointed, Archbishop Charles J Chaput of Denver, Colorado. He was in Toowoomba for a week in late-April 2007. An 'Apostolic Visitator' is a person appointed by the Congregation of Bishops in Rome to examine 'matters relating to the correct exercise of the pastoral function of bishops'. The Visitator examines the diocese and then reports back to the Congregation. It then 'propose[s] to the Supreme Pontiff the appropriate actions to be taken'.[42] Basically this is an administrative procedure set up to deal with particular problems or scandals in dioceses. Since there was no specific problem or scandal in Toowoomba, Chaput's task seemed to be to evaluate Morris' leadership style and ability, as well as examine the state of the diocese and virtually everything else to do with Catholic life in southern Queensland. In other words, Chaput was trawling for whatever he could find. But the underlying issue was the Advent Pastoral.

Chaput has become something of a poster boy for reactionaries among the US hierarchy. What qualifications he had to examine a rural Queensland diocese are yet to be discovered. He arrived in Toowoomba and booked into a motel. All interviews were held in the presence of a priest secretary who sat behind the person or group being interviewed. Chaput demanded secrecy from Morris and the groups and individuals he met. These included various bodies, such as the Council of Priests, the Diocesan Council and the CEO. Individually he spoke to a number of priests, as well as to laypeople who were either supportive or opposed to the policies of the bishop. Chaput struck people as having no real evidence and had very little to say. He was friendly to Morris, and people were courteous to him. The support for Bishop Morris was strong and, with the exception of a few laypeople, unequivocal. Chaput also spoke to Brisbane Archbishop John Battersby who assured him that Morris had the strong support of all the Queensland bishops.[43] Morris did go to Rome in late May and phoned all three congregations involved – Bishops, Worship and the CDF – but received no reply. At the time of publication nothing more has been heard from Rome.

But back to the shortage of clergy. Even an archdiocese like Canberra–Goulburn, which is basically rural with a large urban centre, is facing this problem. There are 55 parishes with 44 diocesan and six religious priests active in parishes. The diocese also has a high proportion of Catholics and the city of Canberra has the best-educated laity anywhere in Australia. In 2005 and 2007 several parishes in Canberra had to be consolidated with the whole of the inner north being combined into one super-parish. A vivid illustration of what has happened in the last 40 years is provided by the Southern Monaro Deanery which takes in southern New South Wales, the Snowy Mountains and the snowfields. In 1961–62 there were two parishes and three priests in Cooma, two priests in Jindabyne, and a parish priest each in Bombala,

Delegate and Adaminaby.[44] In other words eight-and-a-half priests to cover an area that since the mid-1990s has only had three priests. Jindabyne is now a large snowfields town, Thredbo has developed enormously, and during winter the area can have 15000 to 20000 extra people staying over weekends. One priest has to cover the whole of this, plus regular commitments to two country churches. Cooma now has only one priest for the whole town and he has to cover Adaminaby, plus the small towns of Numeralla and Nimmitabel. Delegate no longer has a priest and is covered from Bombala.

One solution to the crisis is to bring in foreign-born priests, mainly from third world countries with apparent surpluses, such as Poland, Sri Lanka, India, the Philippines and parts of Africa. In the diocese of Bunbury in south-west Western Australia just over 70 per cent of the clergy are foreign-born. The archdiocese of Perth also has large numbers and the archdiocese of Brisbane signed an agreement in July 2006 to bring in two priests and four seminarians each year from Nigeria for a pilot program lasting six years. Most dioceses have nowadays adopted this practise.

In the United States, where 16 per cent of priests are foreign born, there has been a study by Dean R Hoge and Aniedi Okure of the results of bringing these priests into parishes.[45] They make the point that the US brought in foreign priests from Europe (Irish, French, German, Italian) right up until the late-1940s, so the authors argue that there is not much that is new about the present influx. However, the situation in Australia is different. Certainly many Irish-born priests and bishops served in Australia up until the 1970s, and in the early decades of the 20th century there were real tensions between the native-born and Irish-born priests. Nevertheless the Catholic community was homogeneously Irish–Australia. There were only limited cultural tensions between priests and people. The situation is different now, as Dr Jane Anderson who has studied this issue has shown.[46] Bringing in priests from countries with very different backgrounds, giving them at best a superficial orientation, and almost immediately placing them in positions of pastoral authority among Australian laity can be problematic. Language and cultural sensitivity issues regularly crop up. The people with whom they deal in parishes are committed Catholics with life-long experience of Australian Catholicism and its transitions since Vatican II, and with behaviourial expectations that are oftentimes not met by the recently-arrived, frequently young, clericalised, and immature priests. Gender relationships are particularly sensitive. Financial accountability can also be an issue. Hoge and Okure correctly point out that foreign-born priests are at best only a 'partial alleviation' of the priest-shortage. They also say that 'the numbers are too low' to cause long-term difficulties in the US.[47] However, this is not true in Australia. Here we have a numerically small group of diocesan clergy who could quickly be out-numbered by too large an influx of non-Australian clergy. This is merely being used by bishops to stave-off a much tougher question: how to deal with the clergy shortage using our own resources. Foreign-born priests are not a real solution to a problem; this can only be solved by the local church.

The priest shortage is not just a question of numbers. It is also a question of the personal and intellectual qualities of the candidates who are presenting for seminary training. Recently an experienced priest–theologian with many years of teaching in Australian seminaries told me he was concerned with the intellectual ability of the candidates accepted into the seminary. He pointed out that some were not capable of tertiary study and that their skills in writ-ten and spoken English were lacking. There are also many students coming into the seminary directly from overseas or applying for seminary-entrance from recently arrived migrant groups. Their lack of command of the English language as well their often low tertiary entrance scores are problematic. Cer-tainly ethnic minority groups are now a sizeable proportion of Mass-going Catholics. Their needs have to be met, but the general tendency among non-Anglo clergy is toward theological conservatism, strong institutional ties and a lack of openness to the broader community.

Some of these impressions have been further clarified by researchers, including Hoge who undertook a follow-up study of priests in the United States ordained between 1996 and 2000, and Mary L Gautier and Mary E Bendyna who specifically studied the men ordained in 2007.[48] These studies showed that ordinands are older on average – from 34.1 to 42.6 years of age for diocesan clergy and 36.8 to 44.2 for religious priests at the time of ordi-nation – that there are a lot fewer of them, that they have to accept heavy responsibility very early in their careers after ordination, that they are less educated and less theologically sophisticated. They tend to work out of a cultic model of priesthood which stresses the essential difference between clergy and laity. Hoge found that they say they are 'happy' in the priesthood and their hero is John Paul II. The reason for this is that they see John Paul pulling 'liberal' Catholics into line and enhancing priestly clericalism and status.

The same profile was outlined by Bishop Julian Porteous formerly of Syd-ney's Good Shepherd Seminary. He says that seminarians enter at a later age, often after a conversion experience. They usually come from smaller fami-lies. Catholicism, he says, provides them with 'a solid grounding and focus for their lives in the midst of a relativised ethical and social culture experi-enced in the world around them'. As in the American research, their hero is John Paul II.[49] Another researcher who has examined this issue is Father Paul Stanosz of the Milwaukee archdiocese.[50] Stanosz says that his research shows

> that we are seeing a decline in the quality of [seminary] applicants ... Many
> of the men in my study entered the seminary in their thirties and forties,
> yet ... they frequently lacked well-developed social and relational skills.
> Many had been away from the church for years before having a conversion
> experience ... today's seminarians are frequently drawn to theologies
> that exalt the status and distinctiveness of the clerical role ... a significant
> number are looking for a religiously saturated environment that will
> bestow a special sense of sacred identity.

In Australia some younger priests tend to see the church in militant terms standing over and against the culture. However, the predominant attitude since Vatican II in mainstream Catholicism has been to offer a coherent cri-tique of society from within it. Sub-cultural, almost sectarian attitudes, create serious concerns as to how these men are going to work in a multicultural, diversified, ecumenical and tolerant Catholic community engaged with the many moral and social issues facing today's church. This doesn't auger well for Catholic intellectual leadership in the future.

It is also worrying that many of these students and priests have either been away from the church for much of their early adult lives, or are actually converts to Catholicism from other faiths or none. A sudden, radical change of life is not a good preparation for ministry, especially if there is not a reasonable period for 'acclimatisation' between conversion and entry into the seminary. This also means that they will have had little or no actual experience of the church as it is lived in Australia and they are often ignorant of the kind of process of change and integration of belief that Catholics who have remained faithful throughout their adult lives have experienced. These men have sometimes returned to Catholicism with an extremely narrow concept of faith after becoming disillusioned with post-modern relativism, and are either consciously or unconsciously determined to 'put right' what they conceive to be theological and moral concessions to secular modernity.

Sociologist Dean Hoge has pointed out that in the US young lay Catholics want a collegial, co-operative church in which the laity play a genuine role in their parish communities. They have little tolerance with status-seeking priests. He has also shown that many younger priests, especially those ordained since the 1990s, take a clerical, non-collegial approach to ministry. He emphasises that 'Research on American priests shows that the youngest diocesan priests are inclined to be less collegial with laity than are older priests. Therefore, the trends among young laity and young priests are divergent. This may produce tension between laity and younger diocesan priests unless communications and discussions are open.'[51] Priest–sociologist Andrew Greeley is typically more blunt. He says that 'Today's young priests tend to want to restore the power that the clergy held not only before Vatican II but also before a large educated laity emerged as a powerful force in the church after World War II.'[52] While the number of young priests like this in Australia is relatively small, there have been examples of communities being decimated by such clergy. One example is a parish in which the priest encouraged lay participation.

When he was moved he was replaced by a recently ordained man in his mid-30s who abolished the sacramental preparation programs and the Rite of Christian Initiation of Adults, sacked the parish council and appointed a new one made up of people not previously prominent in the parish, marginalised the parish sister and drove away most of the regular parishioners, who either gave up or went to a nearby parish.

While there has been quiet discussion going on for a decade among informed Catholics about the psycho-sexual orientation of some seminarians, it was actually the Vatican itself that really brought the issue to public notice. On 4 November 2005 the Congregation for Catholic Education issued an 'Instruction Concerning the Criteria for Discernment of Vocations with Regard to Persons with Homosexual Tendencies'. The Instruction was unequivocal: it distinguished between what it called 'transitory episodes' of homosexuality and 'deep seated' homosexual tendencies. It excluded men from the latter category from ordination. While it decries discrimination against gays, the Instruction says, somewhat inconsistently, that men with 'deep seated' homosexual tendencies are 'intrinsically disordered' and therefore seriously 'obstructed' from relating effectively to men or women. That will come as a surprise to generations of gay priests who have ministered to both sexes successfully in the Catholic church.

Local churches in the English-speaking world, as they usually do, will treat this Vatican Instruction with a fair degree of scepticism. Nevertheless, researchers have been focusing on the increasing number of gay priests in the ranks of the clergy. The church has always had a number of homosexuals in its priestly ranks and in religious orders, and many of them have been extremely successful in pastoral care. Seminary rector and spiritual guide, Father Donald B Cozzens, says that a homosexual orientation of itself doesn't exclude a man from ordination.[53] Cozzens refers to John Boswell's fascinating book, *Christianity, Social Tolerance and Homosexuality*, where the Yale historian argues 'with meticulous scholarship and considerable wit' that from about the 5th century onwards religious orders particularly provided homosexually-oriented men and women with a safe haven from an intolerant and dangerous world.[54] As Cozzens points out, contemporary estimates of the number of gay priests and seminarians vary widely and the simple fact is nobody knows how many there are, but what is clear is that there is a much higher proportion of gays in the present-day priesthood than in the general population. Part of the issue is that a large number of straight priests have left the active ministry over the last 30 years to marry. Also a lot of gay priests have been ordained over the last three decades.

It is clear that the accusation that gay priests are more likely to be child molesters is totally wrong, and lay Catholics have no problem with gay clergy whether they are 'out' or, more likely, quietly integrating their sexual preference. What people find intolerable are the 'closet queens' who, in bouts of self-hatred and denial, are often vicious in their attacks on other homosexual persons demanding all types of punitive measures against them. Self-hating clergy not only destroy themselves, but are much more likely to project their venom outwards and that can lead to extremely rigid and destructive behaviour, especially for vulnerable people in pastoral situations. What the church needs to guard against specifically is admitting this destructive type of person into the seminary. Their rigidity and claims to pseudo-orthodoxy are extremely dangerous and detrimental in pastoral ministry.

So what can be done to save the Australian church from a Eucharistic and sacramental drought? I have already indicated that I consider SWAP services inadequate. If the Vatican and Pope persist in their refusal to allow the ordination of properly trained and appropriate married men and the consideration of a much broader ministry for women, then it is up to the local churches to assume responsibility for their own futures. It would not be the first time that the papacy had to be reformed from outside of Rome. Ultimately this challenge faces all Catholics who have a fundamental right to the regular and reasonably accessible celebration of Mass and the sacraments, and bishops have an obligation to provide that. They also have a fundamental responsibility to provide leadership in the local churches entrusted to them. Their accountability to the papacy must take second place to this primary loyalty. If Rome is unwilling to move, local bishops have to intervene. If not they will stand judged by the Catholic community and by their ordination commitment to the local church.

Visiting Brazil in May 2007, Benedict XVI reasserted the need for celibacy. Addressing the Brazilian Bishops' Conference he said:

> When within the church herself, people start to question the value of priestly commitment as a total entrustment to God through apostolic celibacy and as a total openness to the service of souls, and preference is given to ideological, political and even party issues, the structure of total consecration to God begins to lose its deepest meaning.[55]

It is extraordinary that the Pope thinks that a call for pastoral care of people and a more frequent celebration of the Mass in a country like Brazil with a priest to people ratio of one to 8604 (in contrast to the Assemblies of God where it's one pastor to 35 people) is an 'ideological' and 'political' push.[56] The statistics show why so many Catholics in Latin America are abandoning Catholicism for the Protestant sects: they are simply not being cared for pastorally because of the acute shortage of priests, which itself is created by the demand for celibacy as a precondition for ordination.

When a bishop is ordained he assumes a dual authority and responsibility. His primary responsibility is to the diocese entrusted to him. Secondly he has responsibility to the governance of the universal church and to the maintenance of its unity. Basic to fulfilling his primary responsibility is the provision of Mass and the sacraments. This must come before all other responsibilities. Failure to maintain the sacramental life of the church is a profound dereliction of duty. Thus when Rome insists that a commitment to celibacy is a non-negotiable precondition to ordination, local bishops are placed in an impossible situation. The church is not a centralised, bureaucratic dictatorship. It is communion of local churches and local bishops have the authority to care for their dioceses. But, as I pointed out in *God's New Man*, one of the great tragedies of the Wojtyla papacy was the appointment of bishops who always obeyed Rome and who never stood out or made waves. Talking about US episcopal appointments Andrew Greeley said that the

Vatican appointed 'mean-spirited careerists – inept, incompetent, insensitive bureaucrats, who are utterly indifferent to their clergy and laity'.[57] The large majority of Australian bishops don't fit the Greeley description, although ambition for higher office cannot be excluded in all of them. The majority of our bishops are still very pastoral in their orientation and are concerned about the local church. That is why they now have to take the initiative and focus their attention on the needs of Australian Catholics. Time is running out. The first move needs to be the ordination of married men so that we begin to recover a sufficient number of priests to carry out the ministry. The second step would be to set-up a biblical, theological and pastoral training program that would prepare suitable women and men for ministry. The third step is quite straight-forward: invite back priests who have left the active ministry to fill the gap in the meantime. The overarching context for all of this would be a serious consideration of the meaning of a renewed ordained ministry and the role of women.

This is the real, long-term challenge facing both the church community and the bishops. At present everyone seems to be in a state of compliant paralysis. If Australian Catholics fail to break out of this then the work of the church will grind on for another decade or so, but the heart will have gone out of it, and we will have progressively lost the core of Catholicism; the worship of God and our sharing in the life of Christ through the Mass and the sacraments. If this happens we will no longer be truly Catholic.

4

Why do Catholics leave the church?

People have been coming and going as Catholics since 1788. Some are attracted to the church, while others leave it for varied reasons. The intensity of participation ebbs and flows across a lifetime. So it is difficult to generalise about who is a 'good' Catholic and who is 'bad', and even what these categories mean. Nevertheless it is important to discuss levels of commitment, because that is how we judge success in communicating the message of Jesus.

Mass attendance is a rather rough indicator of commitment, but at least it gives us some basic statistics. This has varied a lot over the last 220 years. If we were to take Catholics in the greater Sydney area in 1833, an informed estimate would be that about 20 per cent attended Mass regularly.[1] A similar percentage attended in 1842. According to Hans Mol's pioneering work *Religion in Australia* this had risen to 22.9 per cent in New South Wales in 1861, to 30.2 per cent in 1881 and to 31.4 per cent in 1901. He says that Victorian Mass attendances were 20.8 per cent in 1861, but then rose to 34.3 per cent in 1881, and 54.3 per cent in 1901.[2] In the last two decades of the 19th century Catholic Mass attendances began to rise, although the discrepancy between New South Wales and Victorian figures is hard to explain. Perhaps it was because Victoria was smaller and more closely settled. While Mol cites lower figures for Anglicans, Methodist attendances were very high, peaking in 1871 at 89.2 per cent.

During the first three decades of the 20th century Catholic practise rates seem to have stabilised around 30 per cent to 35 per cent, and then started to climb again in the years immediately after World War II. Mol says that in 1947 63 per cent of Australian Catholics attended Mass weekly, and that by 1954 this had reached 75 per cent. By 1960 it had dropped back to 53 per cent, only to climb again to 55 per cent in 1962.[3] Since the 1970s these figures have continued to decline, so that by 2001 the attendance rate was 15.3 per cent.[4] My guess is that attendance rates in 2007 stand at about 13 per cent of all Catholics. This will continue to decline because the age profile of attendees is high. What do these figures really tell us? Firstly, the reality is that the decades before the 1860s and the period between federation and World War II were probably the historical norm for religious practise. In pluralist societies like Australia between 20 per cent to 30 per cent of self-identified Catholics on average attend Mass regularly. The figures from between 1945 and 1965 are exceptionally high. The present day attendances are obviously below the average. What is obvious is that it was usually only a minority of Catholics in Australia who took their faith seriously enough to have a real impact on their lives. This led them to attend Mass regularly.

Secondly, the rise from the 1870s onwards is the result of a deliberate decision taken by the majority of the bishops. By this time, a kind of devotional revolution had been foisted on the Irish church by Cardinal Paul Cullen, archbishop of Dublin, and his episcopal allies. This had reached Australia with the appointment to colonial dioceses of a series of forceful Irish bishops from the mid-1860s onwards. These bishops were horrified by 'the laity's half-infidel state' and by the fact that many priests were lazy, often drunkards and occasionally living in concubinage.[5] The bishops thought the situation intolerable and were determined to reform the church, no matter the cost. They were driven by what historian Patrick O'Farrell calls a 'crisis mentality'.[6] Part of this process was setting up a Catholic school system completely without state aid, in response to the secular education Acts in most of the colonies in the 1870s and 1880s. It was a remarkable achievement that only came about because of the availability of religious orders like the Christian, Marist and De La Salle brothers and the Mercy, Josephite and Presentation sisters and other women's orders. Catholic schools became the nurseries of a narrow devotional Catholicism that led to the gradual formation of a sub-culture that subsequently became known after Vatican II as 'ghetto Catholicism'. This was re-enforced with the arrival of the tall, Roman-trained, scholarly and reserved Patrick Francis Moran as archbishop of Sydney in 1884 and his appointment as a cardinal in 1885. Now the intransigent Irish bishops of Australia had a leader.[7]

In November 1885 Moran summoned a Plenary Council, a gathering of all the bishops of Australia and New Zealand, to streamline church structures and impose discipline. The underlying intention was to set narrow devotional and disciplinary parameters for Australian Catholics along Irish lines. The Council issued decrees on a range of topics including clerical discipline, avoiding dangers to faith, Aborigines, marriage, primary and secondary education, literature to be avoided, dancing, male religious and the lives of nuns and religious sisters.[8]

The decrees isolated Catholics and emphasised their 'Irishness'. Supporting this development was the Catholic school system, which by late-1885 was reasonably well established. Priests were instructed that building the school took precedence over constructing a church.[9] But many poor Catholic parents had to be dragooned into sending their children to parochial schools and paying fees. State schools were seen as 'heterodox' where children could lose their faith. Those who refused to send their children to Catholic schools were threatened with refusal of absolution in confession.[10]

The Council's strict legislation on mixed marriages was to be a continuing problem for Catholics and Protestants for the next seven decades, and was explicitly designed to prevent such marriages. The church in the earlier period had been more tolerant because Catholics were a minority and by the 1850s mixed marriages were common. But the take-over of Australia by the Irish bishops meant that Irish custom was to prevail: Catholics married Catholics and Protestants married Protestants. The Council claimed that mixed marriages often led to 'domestic discord, the perversion of the Catholic party and offspring, or what often happens in this country, the children are infected with indifferentism'.[11] Priests were reminded that 'grave and just causes were always required' for a dispensation for a mixed marriage which was to be granted only after *both* parties had promised to bring up the children as Catholics. The marriage was to be celebrated outside the church building (often in the sacristy) without ceremony. Automatic excommunication reserved to the bishop was the penalty for marriage 'before a Protestant [the Latin word used means 'heterodox'] minister or civil official'.[12] The harshness of these terms did untold damage to many people and alienated them from the church. O'Farrell calls it 'a particular abrasion of a day-to-day kind, and at the level of ordinary people'. He also points out that the legislation did not stop mixed marriages and that the resulting interfaith familiarity 'contributed to mutual understanding and tolerance' and that this 'intermix in family and extended family situations … militated strongly against religious segregation and its divisive social effects'.[13]

All of this led to the evolution of a specific style of Catholicism, demanding, self-important and segregated. Those who could not or refused to conform were 'bad Catholics'. For 'good Catholics' it meant submission to clericalism and adherence to strict rules of life that extended from spirituality to the marriage bed. But it gave a sense of superiority, of being better than the common herd. While it was tough as a Catholic, it was also worthwhile and conveyed a sense of dignity, especially if you were a member of the working class and low in the social pecking order, as most Catholics were. At the same time people usually maintained their common sense, and while they may have thought of themselves as 'superior' to their Protestant and ex-Catholic fellow citizens, a strong feeling of commonality bound them to the broader community. This came to the fore particularly during the two world wars. In other words, Catholicism might have been sub-cultural, but it was never a cult. It also had its ugly side. Its bombastic, hierarchical clericalism and refusal to permit independence of mind and freedom of conscience alienated many people. It is often forgotten that this kind of ghetto Catholicism drove many sincere people out of the church, and that sometimes the long-term effects of this faith-style were only realised after Vatican II.

Many who were alienated by the 'old style' only felt free to leave after Pope John XXIII 'opened the windows' of the church.

This is illustrated by the story that follows. It concerns my friend Paul, nowadays a retired Canberra professional, who left the church in the early post-Vatican II period. He was born in 1944 and grew up in the 1950s and his difficulties with Catholicism go back to that period and have little or nothing to do with the post-Vatican II era. He says:

I was once a Catholic, not that I had any say in the matter. I know 'once a Catholic always a Catholic'. Much of it sticks and it's not all bad, but it is great to be free of the bullshit, and there is plenty of that. I am a pre-baby boomer, just. I am the youngest of five and was born into a lower-middle class family in a rural town. I have fleeting memories of my mother; she died before I had a chance to know her. My father took much of his solace for her loss from his religion and it hung over the family like a heavy fog. We lived a few hundred metres from church and school, which was run by the good sisters who were in the 1950s, let us say, uncompromising. Everything revolved around Catholicism. We had a lot of fun and I have many good memories. I never questioned the authority of priests and nuns, not until I reached my mid-teens, anyway.

I don't remember a conscious decision on the matter, but when I was about 15 I started to test the boundaries. There was no mileage in raising issues at home, so the obvious place was religion class. We had a rather old nun, as I recall she was Irish, and clearly not the one to engage in an intellectual discussion on the role of conscience. The simple response I got was either you followed the church's teachings or you went to hell, conscience had nothing to do with it. I clearly recall the frustration in her voice as I continued to pursue my question: what happens if, with a clear conscience, you don't believe. In some ways it was a bit of sport, but I did expect a more reasoned response. The classes degenerated somewhat and ultimately I was banned, but not before I was given six of the best and told I was a disgrace to my dead mother. I was still a committed Catholic then. After all, the church was governed and administered by good and holy people who were doing God's work, and I hadn't long ceased to be an altar boy. I believed that there would be explanations in time. I enjoyed my free periods, often having a cup of tea with the ladies in the canteen, one of whom I remember fondly as sympathetic to me.

After he left home Paul moved to Canberra and joined the public service (this was in the 1960s). At this time he was still a practising Catholic.

It was 10 years before I realised that my kind was not welcome in the church, which only wants compliant people. The break came during the Springboks tour in 1971. The tour was particularly controversial and most countries had suspended sporting contacts with South Africa because of apartheid. The Australian tour went ahead and was confronted by demonstrations everywhere. An opponent of the demonstrators was Archbishop Thomas V Cahill of Canberra–Goulburn. He had written a Pastoral Letter which I heard read at Braddon where I was attending Mass. As I recall it fell short of endorsing apartheid, but it was highly critical of those who opposed the tour, particularly the demonstrators, of whom I was one. It was just too much. In my first letter [to Cahill] I said that the pastoral was tantamount to supporting racism, which I considered inconsistent with the teachings of Jesus. I received a dismissive, patronising response with a smattering of platitudes. In my reply I 'spat the dummy' and said a few things better left unsaid. The reply was short and said something like 'your comments have been noted'. In other words 'piss off'. I now felt that my position in the church was untenable and I would be a hypocrite to stay. Reflecting on these events I realised that I was clinging to the institution that had been an integral part of my life, and I was very reluctant to let go for emotional rather than logical reasons.

On a lighter note, during my attendance at St Patrick's the Redemptorist Fathers came to preach a mission. Throughout the 1950s they had regularly preached missions at my home parish. I can't recall much joy on these occasions. They were about God's wrath on sinners, with lots of souls descending into the eternal flames of hell. Well, the Braddon mission was very different. It was almost as though John and Yoko had been conducting seminars for the Redemptorists. It was all warm and fuzzy, love and forgiveness. But this was strange territory for them; they just couldn't do it. It was embarrassing and I felt sad for them. This episode had some telling messages for me. Like any other business the church was marketing its wares and had to adjust its message to appeal to the target market which had changed. Canberra 1970s was very different to rural Australia in the 1950s. It was much more sophisticated and hell and damnation didn't wash. I also realised the church was essentially a pragmatic organisation. It laid down firm, harsh rules to be observed under the pain of mortal sin, but these could be changed when it suited.

Once having severed my association with the church it was easier to examine objectively some of the issues that I thought were a bit dodgy. These things included the virgin birth, the trinity, transubstantiation, and making a man a god (a very Roman thing to do), not to mention papal infallibility. These were apart from the issues of power and wealth, which had also concerned me for some time.

An example is the current church leadership in Australia. To me the sum of the actions of Cardinal Pell are the antithesis of Jesus. I am thinking of his treatment of gays. I am sure that Jesus would have welcomed them into his company. As I see it Pell is acting at the behest of the Vatican and is not supported by the majority of Australian Catholics. Another example was the vision of John Paul II refusing a priest [Father Fernando Cardenal] in Nicaragua his blessing because he espoused Liberation Theology. The change in the Pope's demeanour when he recognised the priest was stark. He immediately went from the smiling, waving celebrity, to the stern, lecturing autocrat. Well, to me those guys in Latin America are the real Christians doing the hard yards among the poor. The church is not God's church, it is the church of ambitious and ruthless men.

Paul's story is particularly resonant because it not only explains the immediate reason for leaving the church (Cahill's pastoral), but goes into the complex background to the trigger decision. It reflects the stories of other people from the pre-baby-boomer and baby-boomer generations who left Catholicism in the post-Vatican II era. The real reasons were often rooted in the pre-Vatican II church's lack of respect for freedom of conscience, the sometimes bullying or discourteous behaviour of particular bishops and priests, its controlling approach to the community and the inability of its leadership to come to grips with a fast-changing society. Many also left after Vatican II because they felt the church was reacting far too slowly to the challenges of contemporary society and the changes called for by the Council. These people left the church behind as they adapted to contemporary reality, particularly in the sphere of personal morality.

Until recently Catholicism lacked good qualitative research as to why people abandon worship and faith-practise. This lacuna was filled in February 2007 by a Report on *Catholics Who Have Stopped Attending Mass* prepared by the Pastoral Projects Office of the ACBC. The Report focused on people aged from about 25 upward who had given up active participation in the church in the last five years. The Report interviewed 41 people: 28 were women and 13 men, which is about the same ratio as Mass attendees generally. Two-thirds were aged between 40 to 59 and just over half 'had been quite involved or heavily involved in parish life, generally participating in and helping to run a number of programs'. Almost half had attended university and 20 per cent had post-graduate degrees. One-third had not completed tertiary level studies. 'As a group the participants are younger, better educated and far more likely to have been born in Australia than Mass attendees as a whole.'[14] Unlike Paul's experience above, the majority of the people in the Report gradually drifted away from regular Mass attendance.

In the last few decades there has been a continuing collapse in the religious practise of Catholics across all age ranges, but particularly among people from the youngest groups, Generations X and Y.[15] This is vividly shown by the statistics of Sunday Mass attendance over the last decade and a half. The weekly rate in 1996 was close to 18 per cent of all self-reporting Catholics (although it should be remembered that people *over-estimate* the frequency of their attendance at church services). It dropped to 15.3 per cent in 2001, a fall of 100 000 in five years, or 20 000 per year. Even among older Catholics, practise rates are also falling quite sharply.[16] For those aged between 25 and 34 the drop in attendance was double the over-all average with only about 6 to 7 per cent of this age group attending Mass regularly. What is very significant is that nowadays the drop in the number of women attending is roughly equal to that of men, whereas in the past female attendance was always higher.

Another important factor is that 'Around 60 000 of the 775 000 people aged 15 to 24 who had identified themselves (or had been identified by their parents) as Catholics in the 1991 census did not identify themselves that way in the 2001 census, when they were aged between 25 to 34.'[17] So these young people have not just stopped attending Mass; they have stopped identifying themselves as Catholics altogether.

The Report's responses discovered two constellations of reasons: church-centred and participant-centred. While participants were honest about their own failures in commitment, they felt that the fundamental problems with contemporary Catholicism were not personal but embedded within the structure of the church itself. By 'church' they meant the hierarchy. This is illustrated by the first reason the Report highlights: the irrelevance of the church to life today. This was the main reason for 21 participants abandoning regular Mass and was raised as an issue by 40 out of 41 participants. By 'irrelevance' respondents meant that 'the church had lost its ability to connect with the day-to-day lives of ordinary people'. Participants focused on contraception, pre-marital cohabitation, AIDS and condoms, re-marriage and reception of communion after divorce without an annulment, homosexuality, and issues like stem cell research. Celibacy was also often mentioned, the church's leadership was described as 'neither intelligent nor vibrant nor relevant', although local priests were often excused because of their heavy workloads and increasing age. 'What people were saying in a range of ways, was that they could no longer sufficiently locate themselves within the church's world-view to be regular participants in the church's core communal action', the Mass.[18]

A related issue was the misuse of power and authority in the church. People talked about 'disillusionment' resulting from 'lack of consultation and accountability'. Participants felt powerless and didn't believe that anything would change soon. One woman in her 50s said: 'But Jesus who I love and I talk to and pray to and believe in doesn't act like Bishop X and like a lot of those people who to me are just awful people because they are so judgmental and holier than thou and come out and damn people, and publicly. Where's the God there?' The misuse of power was seen in the botched attempts of dioceses to cover-up sexual abuse, the unequal treatment of men and women, particularly the refusal to ordain women, physical abuse and corporal punishment, often many years previously in Catholic institutions and schools, unjust treatment from Catholic employers and dismissal from employment over remarriage without an annulment. An issue that often recurred was the difficulty some people experienced with parish priests. This centred on priestly immorality (eg, sexual abuse of children), or people experiencing 'a priest's behaviour as insensitive, ungracious, rude, arrogant or simply incompetent, or as being out of touch with contemporary Australian life'. People were particularly infuriated by new priests who came into a parish and changed the whole direction of the ministry, particularly from a community-participant model to one in which all authority was focused in the priest, and parishioners were left disenfranchised. 'These problems could be particularly acute if the new priest had come from overseas.'[19]

A number of participants in the Report were put off by the lack of intellectual stimulation at Mass, particularly in sermons. One woman said she didn't have the tolerance to listen 'to what I believe nine times out of ten was drivel'. Another participant said that 'I think it boils down to the fact that the Church is just not smart enough. It really needs some intelligent people running the place.'[20] This highlights the question of the quality of leadership. I pointed out in my 2005 book on Benedict XVI that many poor-quality bishops were appointed during the papacy of John Paul II (1978–2005) and that this would be a challenge for the new pope. 'Given that they had very little sensible episcopal guidance, many Catholics have ended up with a profound sense of a rudderless church lacking any form of credible leadership, so they have simply withdrawn and sought spiritual guidance elsewhere.'[21]

The parish community was important for the Report's participants. When people felt excluded, especially single or divorced people, or where there was poor communication and unkind gossip, or a lack of sincerity, they simply drifted away. Linked to this is a sense of being excluded by canonical rules surrounding remarriage and denial of communion to gays in relationships. As one woman said 'It's not God that's causing the problem, it's the rules and the Church.' Another with a gay daughter added: 'The Catholic Church is quite dishonest. [It] ordains gay men very happily, but then tells us they are all intrinsically disordered and inclined towards evil, so I mean that is such a false dichotomy or a false position.' Another issue was associated with changes in the parish structure, such as merging parishes, changes in Mass times, or the complete withdrawal of a priest from a parish thus forcing the community to have SWAPs.[22]

But not all reasons for abandoning Mass could be sheeted back to the church. A number were personal to the participants. Some of these reasons were external, such as moving to a new area and not connecting with the new parish, mothers who had difficulty getting children to Mass, or looking after them at Mass without support from a husband or partner, and rows and disputes in the family because adolescent children refused to go to Mass. As the children left home some parents felt they no longer had to set an example of Mass practise. Others fell away after the death of a parent. For quite a few people going to Mass was not a priority. Other issues were more important and 'some felt there was just so much else to be done in their lives'. A key issue for many was a crisis of faith. These people felt the church no longer offered them a meaning structure, or its teachings no longer made sense to them. 'The issue for twelve of them was that as adults they no longer found helpful the rigid and rather severe Catholic faith presented to them as children ... They often said that these things prevented them from being able to trust in God and reach a more mature faith.'[23]

Despite all of this, about half of the participants in the Report still attended Mass occasionally and about the same percentage continued to think of themselves as Catholics and about four-fifths still had a connection to Catholicism and faith. They had become 'cultural Catholics'. But they wanted the issues that had driven them away from Mass resolved. Some had become involved with other churches and about three-quarters of them valued spirituality even if it had little to do with the Christian faith and was entirely subjective. Prayer was still important for 76 per cent because it gave them 'a sense of peace and well-being'. Compared to regular Mass attendees many were less likely to affirm unequivocally Christian teachings like the divinity of Christ, the resurrection, the redemption and hell. They also tended to be moral relativists and to see other religions and philosophies as different ways to the same God and truth.[24] The Report also found that 'Many participants displayed a poor knowledge of certain Catholic teachings.'[25] To me, this is significant, because it shows that ignorance of church doctrine goes back into the 'old' system; it is not confined to the post-Vatican II period. In summary, 'The results show that once people stop going to Mass, the degree to which they accept Catholic beliefs and moral teachings is likely to decline … There may be exceptions but, for most Catholics, levels of belief will eventually decline if they do not participate in the life of the Catholic community.'[26] While this may be unwelcome news for the ACBC who commissioned the Report, strategies must be developed to begin to address the issues raised.

A comment needs to be made here on 'cultural Catholicism'. By this I mean people who have ceased practising as Catholics, but who still identify as Catholics and 'whose ethos and attitudes remain generically Catholic, even though their personal adherence to the church many be minimal'.[27] Anglican theologian, Graeme Garrett told me that he thought people still identified as Catholics 'because they don't seem to be held so much by ideas as something more poetic and symbolic, something sacramental … [This is] a cradling and embracing way of thinking, willing and being that you learn not so much with your head, but through other people who already have it and who mediate it to you via nurturing and formation'.[28] This is what the American sociologist Andrew Greeley calls 'the Catholic imagination'.[29] Catholics can 'lose their faith', like Paul in the example above, and be highly critical of the church's doctrinal and institutional structure, but they are still held by a social attachment to the community and by attitudes toward society and social justice by deeper feelings that have more to do with imagination and the way you view life than with reason or doctrine. But there is a serious question as to whether cultural Catholicism has been handed on to the next generation.

So having seen why previous generations have abandoned the practise of Catholicism, we now move on to perhaps the greatest dereliction of the church in the last 30 years: the failure of the Catholic community to hand on the faith to Generations X and Y, that is people between late adolescence and the late-30s. These are the children and grandchildren of the baby boomers. The sad fact is that the vast majority of Generations X and Y know little or nothing about their faith and probably more than 80 per cent of them will have ceased practising by late-adolescence and eventually they will lose contact with the church, even though they may still call themselves 'Catholic'. There is also an increasing number of Generations X and especially Y who have given up the church altogether, and no longer identify as Catholics.

Again we are lucky to have a major, national three-year research project on the spirituality of young Australians which has resulted in a book, *The Spirit of Generation Y: Young People's Spirituality in a Changing Australia*.[30] The project was sponsored by the Australian Catholic University and Monash University. This project defined Gen Y as people born between 1981 and 1995 and interviewed young people from many religious backgrounds and none.[31] One of the key issues facing the researchers was the definition of 'spirituality'. They defined it as 'a conscious way of life based on a transcendent referent'.[32] In other words they tried to elicit how people made sense of their lives, what meaning-structure and contextual ethos they used to give themselves purpose and direction, the context in which they operated. It is clear that there are three basic spirituality 'types' represented among Gen Y. The first group is traditionally religious, that is they have accepted traditional formulations of faith based on Christian teachings, or the other major faiths. Forty-six per cent fit into this category. Twenty-eight per cent were classified as secular or humanist, that is their worldview was formed by experience and reason and they were secular and non-religious in their approach to life. Seventeen per cent had embraced an 'eclectic' or new age type of spirituality and 9 per cent fitted the 'other' category.[33]

Perhaps what is more significant is that 80 per cent of Gen Y believe that there is 'something out there', and 70 per cent actually believe that this something or somebody actually cares about us; this group includes many of those who are classed as humanists. Twenty-two per cent of respondents unhesitatingly believe in God. These figures are significant because it shows that young people are not the absolute 'heathen' they are sometimes made out to be by their elders. Lead researcher and priest, Father Michael Mason, told Radio National that

> the statistic that's very often quoted is that only 48 per cent of Generation Y believed in God. Well that's a little bit misleading. There were another 30 per cent who said they were unsure … it turns out two-thirds of them said they believed in some kind of higher being … and most of those believe that this higher being or life force cares about us.

Mason also said that Gen Y 'think it's fine to pick and choose among the various beliefs that make up their religion, they tend to agree that moral values are relative, that there are no absolute rights and wrongs for everybody'.[34]

Clearly there is still a consciousness among the young of a somewhat undifferentiated transcendent 'out there'. However, this doesn't transfer into an identification with a denomination. The survey research shows that Gen Y's actual connection with the church is somewhat lower than the 2006 census figures would suggest. In the case of Anglicans it is 6 per cent lower than in the census and Catholics are 5 per cent lower. The percentage in the Gen Y survey stating 'no religion' was 13 per cent higher for this age group than stated in the 2006 census.[35] What is important from the church's perspective is that the research reveals 'quite dramatic losses of young members by the Anglican and Catholic churches' to the 'no religious identification' category. In other words Gen Y members are giving up on the mainstream churches in large numbers.[36] What is even more significant is that nowadays young women are no more religious than young men and abandon the church in the same proportions. The reasons for abandoning membership were complaints about the church (one said 'Primary school was a Catholic school and I witnessed the hypocrisy and I am not impressed with the general history of the church'), moral teaching ('They teach Jesus accepted everyone but they don't accept gay people'), beliefs ('Impossibility from a science perspective of the things referred to in the bible'), religion as a means of controlling people's lives, problems with belief in God ('I'm not sure I believe in God – I don't believe in the resurrection of Jesus'), and the inability to reconcile suffering and the goodness of God. The researchers concluded that 'one quickly forms the impression that those who no longer identify with a religion are people who have 'issues' with the church – mostly the Catholic and Anglican churches'.[37]

One of the most interesting conclusions the researchers reached was that spiritually and religiously Gen Y young people are very similar to their baby boomer parents, but – and this is the important difference – they have reached scepticism about faith and the church at a much lower age. The researchers believe that the long-term result of this will be that 'Gen Y will contain many fewer Christians by the time they are thirty years older.'[38] Significantly Gen Y have a deeper consciousness of God relating to us as a person than their parents and are 'less likely to find it OK to pick and choose one's beliefs', that is they are paradoxically more orthodox in these matters than their parents. Nevertheless they are still likely to agree that morals are relative.[39] The Christian groups that scored highest on every measure of Christian belief and practise among Gen Y were Lutherans, Churches of Christ, Baptists, Pentecostals and evangelicals. These young people are more likely to attend church services, to feel close to God, believe in the divinity and resurrection of Jesus and pray frequently. The researchers tried to explain this 'trend-bucking' phenomenon and asked themselves: 'Is the style of religiosity of these denominations particularly well suited to youth, and less so to adherents as they age?' or 'are we seeing the results of effective evangelistic campaigns?', or a combination of the two?[40] The answer is probably the latter.

This work on Gen Y has been supported by independent research by Dr Philip Hughes of the Christian Research Association. According to Hughes the majority of young people who do attend church as teenagers say that church communities are generally warm and accepting, but that the services are boring and not relevant.

More than eighty per cent of young people believe there could be a spiritual dimension to life. But less that ten per cent have actively explored religions and spiritualities other than the Christian faith ... For most young people life revolves around ... friends and family and in excitement-generating activities. They value music greatly and often turn to music to express themselves, to reflect or to change their moods ... Many see the way to an enjoyable life through success in their studies or finding an interesting job.

They are uncertain about belief and what life is about and they are unwilling to accept the authority of church or school and want to make decisions for themselves. New age beliefs appeal to some and a third are unsure about whether there is a God.[41]

Although this is a seemingly contradictory trend (logic and consistency is not normally a characteristic of human behaviour), there is also evidence that the young tend to think that it is important that authority figures like the pope and the bishops proclaim Christian morality strongly as an ideal toward which everyone should strive. That is why they cheer the pope at WYDs and say they want clear rules, even if they have no intention of keeping them themselves. WYDs are an example of what Emile Durkheim, calls 'collective representation'. This is when people are pleasantly surprised to find themselves part of something bigger and more universal than themselves, and discover that they all share a common spiritual ethos and purpose. On these occasions they look for a statement of identity and clearly articulated ideals and moral values, almost like 'categorical imperatives'. As a leader-figure at WYDs, the pope symbolises the collective and articulates the ideals. Needless to say, many will most likely not apply to themselves the moral values laid down, but they still want to hear them. They seem blithely unaware of the disjunctive nature of that kind of behaviour. So while Gen Y may cheer the pope, they will certainly make their own decisions about sexual activity and the way they live out their gender identity.

Some from Gen Y have rejected the more open, self-directed moral decision-making offered them by their parents, their education, post-modernism and society at large. To some extent this probably reflects their rebellion against the openness shown by the generation before them (who wanted to let the young make their own choices). Some in Gen Y seem to be saying relativity has its limitations, because they are left with no certainty and their lives seem to be built on shifting sands. They at least want to know about traditional moral values, even if they largely ignore them in their own lives.

Interestingly, according to a longitudinal study that began in 1981 of European Catholic and Protestant youth, a minor religious renewal seems to have occurred in Western and especially Eastern Europe, that to some extent parallels Australia. In Europe there is an interest among the young in spirituality and belief in God and life after death, even as church attendance continues to fall and fewer are turning to the church for answers. Nevertheless, many young people have stronger religious beliefs than 20 years ago. Even among European youth who describe themselves as 'without religion', belief in God has jumped from 20 per cent in 1981 to 29 per cent in 1999.[42] In Eastern European countries and in Italy and Portugal (but not in Ireland) both rates of belief and church attendance among the young are rising. Nevertheless the Catholic theologian, Pierre de Locht of the Catholic University of Leuven, warns that this doesn't mean they will flock back to the churches.

> Youth no longer have confidence in the church as an institution. First
> because its moral positions are too rigid and don't correspond to
> today's problems. And also because the church wants to keep a sort of
> institutionalised monopoly on faith, which doesn't acknowledge individual
> expression.[43]

It is interesting to compare young Australians with their counterparts in the United States. US Catholic sociologist Andrew Greeley has shown that Generation Y want to remain in the church, even if they don't necessarily practise their faith. Nevertheless 85 per cent of them favour married priests and the ordination of women, 75 per cent advocate that divorced-remarried Catholics be able to receive communion, 65 per cent support contraception and, he might have added, more than half support abortion in certain circumstances.[44] Greeley has also shown that these figures represent the view of all Catholics in developed countries and that while the power of the papacy is at an all-time high, the popes have simply failed to impose the old rules of sexual behaviour on Catholics. But Greeley argues that no matter what happens – including the child sexual abuse crisis – it is very hard to drive Catholics out of their heritage. This possibly reflects the US situation more than the Australian, although there is also a strong residual 'cultural Catholicism' present here.

Another recent book on US Catholics, *American Catholics Today*, found that 'Never before in history have we had Catholic young adults so highly educated, so well informed, so well traveled, so aware of cultural differences, so determined to think for themselves, and so affluent, as we have today ... They are religious, but in a different way [from their elders].' The research found that those born after 1961 emphasised a reliance on personal conscience and individualism, that they wanted to participate in church decision-making and that they took a 'situational' approach to issues of sex and gender, that is the morality of a particular action involving sexuality was more determined by the situation in which the individual found themselves than by abstract notions of morality.[45] Speaking on Radio National's *Religion Report* one of the authors, Dean Hoge, said that contemporary young Catholics

> are the most educated and the most culturally aware, and maybe the most capable of any young Catholics in [US Catholic] history ... We may say they're not as good Catholics, but they're very impressive people, and they think for themselves. So they have a feeling of entitlement to make many decisions about religion and morality and life for themselves, and therefore church authority is not honoured as much as it was in the last generation.[46]

To balance this somewhat optimistic picture other surveys find that among American youth more generally, the evidence is that while young people want to identify with a church, that doesn't mean they know anything specific about the beliefs, commitments and theology attached to Christianity, or that they even think that these are important. In the USA, the young tend to see God as a kind of 'cosmic therapist' and 'divine butler'. In other words, God is there to heal your hurts and is always ready to be called on to assist you when you need 'divine help', such as passing an exam or getting a partner. These conceptions are self-centred and probably also reflect youth in Australia.

The conclusion of all of this evidence is that Australian young people today face a bewildering multiplicity of choices regarding 'meaning systems' and 'world views'. They embrace, jettison or combine them according to what is important to them in the process of finding their own identity. They tend to view everything presented to them with a kind of detachment and ask 'What's in it for me?', or, at a more elevated level they ask 'How does it fit into my quest to find myself, to discover who I am?' Religious sociologist Michael Mason says that they live in a profoundly secular world without ideals and visions to capture their imaginations. 'There's a fear of illusion in Australian culture that's almost led us to being reluctant to dream ... You could perhaps characterise Generation Y as being the first to be young in a culture that doesn't trust dreams or visions.'[47] This leaves them in a kind of arid world with a rather thin sense of their own identity and an even more tenuous sense of the community to which they belong.

Yet here also lies one of Catholicism's great counter-cultural strengths. Nowadays it is often in the Catholic school rather than the family that children and young people are taught the importance of community and where they learn that the individual must act with justice and integrity and that each has a responsibility towards others. It is here that they are offered a critique of individualism, self-obsession and consumerism. Unless they come from a seriously committed Catholic family, the school is the place where the young are initiated into the imaginative world of Catholicism, a world in which there is a sense of the transcendent presence of God, where symbols have meaning and where love, hope, forgiveness, and care for others are the primary ethical norms. Andrew Greeley has been arguing for years that this is why Catholic schools are so important: 'They are resources in social capital that the church should treasure, and they are more important in a time of change in the church than in a time of stability.'[48] I will return to this in the next chapter.

There is also a sense in which emphasis on the numbers of Gens X and Y who have abandoned Catholicism is misleading. It lacks the kind of historical context provided at the beginning of this chapter. People have been coming and going in Catholicism for centuries. While it may have been dangerous in medieval Europe to declare oneself a non-believer or be declared a heretic because both these stances were socially deviant, there has been increasing tolerance of diverse approaches to belief since the late-17th century and the 18th-century Enlightenment. It also needs to be remembered that since the end of the Roman persecutions and the reign of Emperor Constantine the Great (306–337), serious commitment to the faith has always been a minority affair in the sense that only the true believers lived a full Christian life; the majority remained at a nominal level of dedication. The most optimistic estimate is that historically only about one in 10 Catholics have ever really lived the demands of love, forgiveness, charity and commitment to God laid down by Christ in the gospels in any serious sense. So at best Catholicism has always had only a minority actively living their faith.

What seems to have happened today is that many of this elite minority from Gens X and Y who in the past might well have joined religious orders or the priesthood, or been the lay leaders in the church, are nowadays involved in various movements demanding serious, even radical commitment. For instance many are involved in environmentalism, or working for social justice either in Australia or overseas, or seriously searching for a meaning or purpose in life involving a commitment to others, such as serving the homeless or working for organisations like L'Arche. Phillip Adams constantly comments on *Late Night Live* on ABC Radio National that many of the people he works with in social justice projects are Catholics, especially priests and sisters. Personally I have had a long involvement in environmentalism and it has often struck me that many of the most committed young activists, the ones who literally put their bodies on the line to protect the natural world, came from Catholic schools or from a Christian background. At first I was inclined to treat this as my bias: you see what you want to see. But William Lines, the author of *Patriots*, the most comprehensive study of the Australian environmental movement since 1945, asked me out of the blue one day why there were so many Catholics in the environmental movement.[49] I think the answer is that, at its best, a Catholic or Christian education emphasises community responsibility, a sense that we don't just live for ourselves, that social justice demands a commitment to equity and to caring for others and a willingness to sacrifice the self for the greater good. At a deeper, unconscious level, faith education gives people the facility to perceive that living things are sacred and point beyond themselves. In other words, this is an education that creates a broad, spiritual context and a deeper sense of the meaning of life.

It was precisely this that inspired earlier generations of young Catholics to dedicate their lives to God and the service of others. Now it inspires young Catholics to become activists. Some think that this is a great loss to the church. I don't. It is a gift to the wider society, which perhaps needs these people more than the church.

5

How should the church respond?

So how should the church respond? We have partly answered this question in Chapter 4. But what else needs to be done? How should Catholicism's most important ministries, parishes and schools respond? Can the church try to stem the numbers leaving? Should it? And how do you proclaim the gospel in modern Australian society?

Before we tackle these questions, we need to remember that Catholicism doesn't exist for its own sake, the church is not an end in itself. Its mission is to worship God, to celebrate the Eucharist and the sacraments, to proclaim God's Word and kingdom through the person and message of Christ, and to minister through serving others and working for genuine justice and equity in society, as well as confronting personal and structural evil. Catholics believe that it is God's Spirit that inspires Catholicism and, while still guaranteeing human freedom, guides the church to the extent that it will not ultimately lose its way and abandon the message of Jesus. In other words the Spirit writes straight with our crooked lines. This is the church's mission statement.

There is already a spectrum of responses as to how Catholicism should carry out its mission in Australia. Before we consider that spectrum we need to remember that many in the church are wearied by the endless struggles between 'conservatives' and 'progressives'. There is a real sense in which we are in the *post*-post-Vatican II period. In this phase we deal with different interpretations of what happened at Vatican II. A small number of people have rejected the Council, the so-called 'traditionalist' Catholics. Some of these would have joined the Lefebvrist schism (a group who follow the French archbishop Marcel Lefebvre) and have broken with the mainstream church, but not all of them. Tiny pockets of hard-line traditionalists still exist within Catholicism. However, the vast majority of Catholics have embraced the reforms of the Council and, as we have already seen many from the Vatican II generation feel frustrated by the failure of the hierarchy to embrace the kind of structural reform that would incorporate the new vision of the church.

As the research outlined in the previous chapter makes clear, most younger Catholics know little and care less about all of this. The only Catholicism they have known is the post-Vatican II version, but many of them have little sympathy with ecclesiastical culture wars over interpretations of the Council. To re-involve them, Catholicism will have to present a vision of faith that captures the ideals that appeal to their imaginations and convictions. As the theological saying goes, 'grace builds one nature': that is God's Holy Spirit depends on our wisdom, intelligence and ability to present Catholicism in a way that engages people and prepares them to hear the Word of God. Catholics believe that as the church responds to contemporary challenges God's Spirit becomes active. But even that doesn't guarantee that what we decide to do will necessarily be correct. In order to make a right decision we need as much objectivity and research as we can muster.

The way Catholics respond to contemporary challenges will depend on which part of the theological spectrum they inhabit. By placing everyone on a spectrum we recognise that *all* are Catholics and that they all have contributions to make in building up the church. We all need to get beyond stereotypes and recognise the sincerity and contribution to the rich fabric of the church of Catholics with different attitudes to our own, even if we personally don't agree with their specific emphasis. The reason why I stress this is because I have so often been told by Catholics who disagree with me to 'get out and found your own church if you can't accept the doctrines and rules of the club!' Such people believe that their very narrow definition of Catholicism is the only one that is valid; everyone else is a 'heretic' and beyond the pale.

Talk about this divide in terms of 'conservative' and 'progressive' is deceptive because most Catholics have moved beyond these categories. American journalist and Vatican specialist, John Allen, has suggested that a way around these words is by acknowledging two schools of thought in Catholicism. One emphasises change, the other continuity. The change school tends to see Vatican II as a decisive break with the religious attitudes of the past, while the other school focuses on the links and the continuity between Vatican II and the pre-1960s church.[1] The reality is more complex, but the advantage of these terms is that they allow all mainstream Catholics to be included in the modern church. Contemporary Catholics constellate around attitudes to the world, history, contemporary culture, and the church's relationship to all three. The way you view reality and your place in culture tends to determine the way you view Catholicism.

So how do we define this spectrum across Catholicism?

At one end are those who tend to focus on the world as a sinful place and humankind as a fallen race tainted with original sin. They despair about postmodern culture teaching us anything worthwhile. These are the people who want the church to stand-up and offer a critique of the world and soon-to-be forgotten political correctness. If, like Benedict XVI, you see the church as the sole repository of absolute, unchangeable truth about God, life and moral values, then your response to the ministerial dilemmas Catholicism faces will be to say that the church is here to guide the world and that it has little or nothing to gain from mundane wisdom. The Catholic's task is to tell it as it is, to proclaim the church's teaching in season and out of season. This is especially true regarding life issues like abortion, stem cell research and contraception, and gender issues like homosexuality, which are seen as centrally important in today's world. The church should batten down the hatches, tighten up on discipline, consolidate inwardly, and confront the world with the 'hard' teachings of Jesus. Actually, more accurately, the 'hard' teachings of the papal magisterium, which are then identified with Jesus. To these people the universal church is strongly linked with the papacy. In terms of worship, these Catholics emphasise the importance of the sacred. Liturgy is about entering the presence of God; this requires an attitude of silent adoration and an emphasis on musical and artistic beauty. This should be reflected through the language used and the deportment of worshipers.

However, if you have a more positive, optimistic view of the world as revealing something of God's goodness, if like John XXIII, you can perceive what is worthwhile in modern culture and if you feel that history itself is part of the ongoing revelation of God, then you will be at the progressive end of the spectrum. Such Catholics believe that while the world is grace-filled with God's presence and the church is one of the most important ways through which people have access to truth and to an experience of God, there is also a recognition that there are other ways to God, which are found in so many great religious traditions. In order to achieve its goal the church must be part of culture, it must emphasise those aspects of its teaching that best respond to the particular needs of the time and place. The focus is on the local church. While maintaining an open stance toward the contemporary world, the church must also offer a direct and honest critique, derived from the Scriptures, of modern culture and values. But it must also be willing to participate in the world, to learn from it and to co-operate with other people of good will in building the structures of love, mercy and justice. The church and its structures are themselves subject to sin and failure, the papal magisterium has at times been wrong, and that the sins of its members infect the very structure of Catholicism itself. For people at this end of the spectrum openness and ecumenism are key values and a strong assertion of Catholic identity is not so important. The predominant leitmotif of the progressive is a sense of living in history with its changing realities and values. In terms of worship these Catholics embrace the community aspect of liturgy.

The extremes of both of these positions are, of course, caricatures, and most people don't hold either of them in their entirety. While there is a lot of crossover between the two, there is no doubt that we all *tend* toward one or the other end of the spectrum as much according to our psychology and experience as from our intellectual convictions. Clearly I belong at the more change-oriented end of the spectrum and Cardinal George Pell belongs at the more continuity-oriented end. An issue that has recently focused the differences between the two is the primacy of conscience in individual moral decision-making. Freedom and reliance on conscience tend to be strongly stressed by those who are change-oriented. By contrast these attributes are questioned or sometimes denied by those focused on continuity. While I would see primacy of conscience as the ultimate moral guide for the individual Christian, Pell recently said that it is 'incompatible with traditional Catholic teaching' and added that 'even in Catholic circles, the appeal to primacy of conscience is being used to justify what we would like to do rather than what God wants us to do'.[2]

These stances are not mutually exclusive. Worship is one topic where some at the progressive end, including myself, recognise that while welcoming people and making them feel part of the community at the Eucharist and sacraments is important, we also need to recover some sense of the sacred and the beautiful. Sensible people realise that there is truth in both perspectives. The key issue is where you place your emphasis. Theology is not so much about incompatible views as about what aspects of revelation you think are important.

But the tragedy is that at present there is still an enormous amount of antagonism between the two emphases. Numerically the continuity group in Australia is fairly small, probably at most about 10 per cent of all Catholics. Many supporters of the Latin Mass would be part of this group. This group is strongly committed, so it punches well above its weight and is quite influential both in its connections with a few of the bishops and the Vatican. The problem with change-oriented people is that they are not politically astute and many have given up their active commitment to Catholicism and are simply standing on the sidelines. In the US the situation is more fraught with the two sides resembling armed camps.

What needs to be recovered from the tradition is what the New Testament calls *koinonia* or the 'spirituality of communion'. Essentially this means that all believers share in communion with God and each other through their baptism into the body of Christ and their membership of the church. All have gifts given uniquely to each by the Holy Spirit which they can contribute to the community and through it the wider world. In that way what Saint Paul in First Corinthians (chapter 12) calls 'the body of Christ' can operate at an optimum with everyone contributing their gifts in communion with the gifts of others. In New Testament theology it is the Holy Spirit that guides all these gifts and gives them cohesion. *Koinonos* is one of those rich Greek words which means a companion, partner or joint owner. In the New Testament context the word is used to describe the relationship that 'binds Christians to each other, to Christ and to God'.[3] It involves a sharing in friendship that builds up the Christian community and strengthens common faith, and it is a reaching out towards others. At its deepest level, it is a fellowship in the Spirit of Christ and a communion with God through the sacrament of the Eucharist in which the Christian shares in the very body and blood of the Saviour. In the earliest Christian community it was lived out in an almost communistic style of existence:

> They [the Christian converts] devoted themselves to the apostles' teaching and fellowship, to the breaking of bread and the prayers ... All who believed were together and had all things in common; they would sell their possessions and goods and distribute to all, as any had need. Day by day they spent much time together in the temple. They broke bread at home ... praising God and having the goodwill of all the people [Acts of the Apostles 2:42–47].

This fellowship doesn't exist in the contemporary church. While the ideological divides in Australia are not quite as bad as in the US, there is little or no communication across the spectrum. Change-oriented Catholics feel the continuity group have control of the resources of the institutional church. However, this picture does an injustice to many of the other Australian bishops who take a very pastoral approach and have much in common with the change-oriented group. As we've seen in the case of Toowoomba's Bishop William Morris (see Chapter 3) many bishops have shown courage and leadership in their dioceses where they have often had to deal with aggressive and divisive groups whose *ad hominem* attacks can be withering. The Queensland bishops are stand out examples of a pastoral approach, but they are not alone. The word 'pastoral' is often read as meaning 'progressive', which is not accurate. 'Pastoral' in this sense means bishops care about people and they understand that while Christian ideals and living Catholicism in integrity is challenging and important, people often fail. But that doesn't mean that they should be abandoned. A pastoral bishop is one who reaches out to the whole community and who works for reconciliation. The model is the forgiving father in the parable of the prodigal son in Saint Luke's gospel, the loving parent who embraces his returning son who has 'devoured [the father's] property with prostitutes' (Luke 15:30).

Ironically the identification of 'pastoral' with 'progressive' means that many continuity-oriented people feel that they are neglected because they often argue they have little influence in the bureaucracy of the church, except in a few dioceses. This is certainly the impression you get reading the magazine *AD2000*. Its editor, Michael Gilchrist, complains in his book *Lost!* that '[e]ven during the long pontificate of John Paul II many ineffectual appointments [of bishops] were made to Australian dioceses ... The settled view among these bishops, along with their bureaucrats, clergy, religious and assorted minders appears to be that watered-down, cafeteria-style 'lite' Catholicism is a fact of life' and that to challenge this line 'can actually put at risk one's position or livelihood.'[4] This is a little like a major party claiming the underdog status in an up-coming election. Gilchrist says that these 'ineffectual' bishops are those whose style is 'more tolerant, inclusive, open to new ideas, democratic in outlook, slow to censor. Bishops with these ... qualities were called 'pastoral'.'[5] Gilchrist is also very concerned about 'a few "empowered", liberal-minded activists'. I'm glad he said 'few' because, search as I might, I find it hard to discover these well-organised people 'trapped as they are in their 60s and 70s time warp and spiritual blinkers'.[6]

In fact what the Americans call Catholic 'reform groups' are minuscule in Australia without institutional influence. Efforts by those from the reformist end of the spectrum produced the webpage *Online Catholics* in mid-2004, but it folded in early-2007 due to lack of financial backing, and even the

Jesuit-supported *Eureka Street* has had to switch to an online format to survive. One of the more hopeful signs is that not long before *Online Catholics* folded, publisher Brian Coyne launched a new online news and opinion magazine, *Catholica Australia*, which breaks stories and offers a moderately critical appraisal of the church in Australia.

One organisation that has tried to build some bridges across the spectrum is Catalyst for Renewal (with its magazine *The Mix*), which was started by a number of prominent Sydney Catholics in July 1994. Despite a well-articulated vision and the work of Father Michael Whelan as executive director, it too has run-up against the problem of funding and lack of institutional support. There is only so much a group of individuals can do. However, 'Spirituality in the Pub' (which the organisation established) is still going strong. People, often in groups of several hundred, get together in a hotel to hear speakers from various points of view talk on theology, ethics, or social issues. Essentially the problem for all of these groups is that it is hard for volunteers to maintain momentum, let alone find the finance to cover costs without any institutional support.

The Catholic community in Australia is much smaller than in the USA; this may prove to be a great strength. Because there are less of us, the task is not so Herculean; people can more easily meet and get to know each other. Perhaps another strength is that Australians tend to live and let live. But one of the fundamental problems, even if we could get people together, is to find a commonly accepted set of assumptions and even a common language. It is possible to attain common ground especially on issues like worship, traditional Catholic spirituality and the need to recover some sense of the sacred. Only when you have established this can you begin to build a personal relationship. Once you have achieved that, dialogue is easier.

One of the most difficult issues is that people from both sides of the spectrum often don't really know or understand either theology or the Catholic tradition. They are what Father David Jaeger calls 'gut' conservatives and 'gut' liberals' without any knowledge of church history, doctrine, or the dynamics of belief.[7] This means that even when you get people talking and working together, it is hard to find common ground because each end of the spectrum tends to emphasise different priorities. For one side it's social justice, for the other life issues. If 'gut' believers do have any theological learning or have read any church history it will tend to be narrow and used to support their own point of view, which they take to be normative. What tends to happen is that 'ideological simplicities' rule supreme.[8] Getting beyond mere caricatures of each other's position is often a difficult hurdle and it is hard to know how you give people knowledge and understanding without them being willing to undertake adult religious education and theological training. Nevertheless there is still enough agreement within Catholicism about God, Christ, the Holy Spirit, the creed and the Eucharist and sacraments, to sustain common meaning and a ground for dialogue. The contentious areas are the nature of the church, authority, conscience and morality, but even here the church has spanned centuries, cultures, languages and political systems without splitting apart. In fact church history is probably Catholicism's most optimistic symbol. As I keep repeating in this book, a church that has persisted through crisis after crisis for two millennia has clearly developed remarkable survival skills. No doubt these are still operative.

It is clear is that leadership is a key issue here, and this is one area where Benedict XVI has intervened decisively. He personally supervises the appointment of bishops. He looks for men of some intellectual quality, although he doesn't always succeed in finding them. Vatican commentator, Sandro Magister says that Benedict 'maintains that a rebirth of the church and its purification must come from a new generation of more motivated and energetic bishops'.[9] Benedict no longer leaves the process to Cardinal Giovanni Battista Re, the prefect of the Vatican's Congregation of Bishops who, in the last years of the John Paul II papacy had *carte blanche* in episcopal appointments. As I showed in detail in *God's New Man* some disastrous appointments were made during the last papacy, including that of Cardinal Hans Herman Gröer to Vienna who turned out to have a long history of sexual abuse of junior students for the priesthood. Several of the bishops nominated were mentally unstable.[10] There were other appointments of men lacking even basic leadership skills and breadth of vision.

Benedict is right. It is the bishops who have to begin to show the kind of leadership that will draw Catholicism together and bring about 'a unity in the work of service' (Ephesians 4:12) as the Jerusalem Bible translation puts it. The bishop has to be the catalyst and the one who promotes dialogue in his diocese, being authoritative without being authoritarian, acting as a bridge between people. The word 'bridge' is significant here because it is one of the bishop of Rome's many titles, in this case taken from the pagan priesthood where the head priest – and later the emperor himself – was the *Pontifex maximus*, the supreme bridge-builder between heaven and earth. The idea here is that bishops are called to bridge the chasms that separate people in their communities and dioceses.

In many ways the majority of the Australian bishops have tried to hold different groups of Catholics together. In the last few decades they have generally taken a reconciling stance. They have tried to stand above the ruck, to tolerate differences of approach and support pastoral care for all. There has been a willingness to allow diverse approaches to Catholicism. However, their confidence was badly dented at the time of the Synod for Oceania in late-1998 when they were out-maneuvered by a tiny group of reactionary laypeople who, with the tacit support of a few of the bishops, had complained endlessly for a number of years to Rome about the 'parlous state' of doctrinal orthodoxy and 'pastoral deviations' in Australian Catholicism. They were particularly concerned with liturgical practise, especially the use of the third rite of reconciliation. This is when a general confession of sin is made by the community and an absolution covering everyone at a worship service is granted. This occurs instead of specific confession to an individual priest. On return to Australia, after being chastised by the Vatican via a very critical 'statement of conclusions', the bishops faced a great deal of public criticism and the impossible situation of having to choose between loyalty to Rome and their commitment to the local church.[11] While some supported the Roman line publicly, most of them retreated into a kind of sullen silence. Things have settled down since then, but the challenge is still there for the bishops, as it is on a parochial scale for priests: to provide genuine Christian leadership.

The New Testament has much to say about this and it is lived and modelled by Jesus himself in the gospels, especially when he washes the feet of his apostles at the last supper.[12] In Saint John's gospel (13:3–15) he says: 'So if I, your Lord and Teacher, have washed your feet you ought to wash one another's feet.' It is clear that the New Testament norm of leadership is significantly different to that of the political world. Jesus is absolutely clear, telling his followers: 'You know that the rulers of the Gentiles lord it over them, and that their great ones are tyrants over them. It will not be so among you; but whoever wishes to be great among you must be your servant, and whoever wishes to be first among you must be your slave; just as the Son of Man came not to be served but to serve' (Matthew 20:25–28). Saint Peter reflects the same message in his First Letter, written possibly in the year he was martyred in the persecution initiated by the Emperor Nero (AD64). Peter advises his fellow presbyters (bishops in our terms) never to 'lord it over those in your charge, but be examples to the flock'. In the light of these texts the church's constant struggle throughout its history ought to have been to avoid secular political models of power and to have exercised a form of servant leadership which involves the self-effacing task of helping others to discern their gifts, creating an ambience for their use, supporting them in their ministries and drawing the whole together to give a sense of unity and direction to the work of the church. This is no easy task and in many ways the church has failed seriously as it adopted various political models borrowed from the surrounding culture as its form of government.

In order to break out of this Catholic leaders, whether they be pope, bishop, priest or layperson, will increasingly need to recover and integrate Jesus' and the New Testament's model of leadership as service. Certainly they would be helped by training in listening and dialogue, as well as group process and facilitation. They will also need considerable maturity and experience and those who are uncertain about their own identity, or who have low levels of tolerance or self-esteem, or who are easily frustrated, or who tend to dominate others, or who are psycho-sexually immature, are unsuited to any leadership role. The personal qualities of those chosen as bishop are as important as, or perhaps more important, than doctrinal orthodoxy. It is precisely these leadership qualities that were often ignored throughout the long papacy of John Paul II when complete loyalty to Rome was the prime virtue. There is little evidence that Benedict is taking the issue of leadership ability seriously either, although as we saw, he at least values intelligence and theological sophistication.

The gift of genuine leadership is one of those intangible qualities that is difficult to define, but involves the subtle ability to encapsulate within oneself the ethos and élan, the spirit and inner heart of what it is they represent. Somehow John XXIII, Martin Luther King Jn, John F Kennedy, Nelson Mandela, Burma's Aung San Suu Kyi and even Winston Churchill possessed this intangible but recognisable quality. In other words the genuine leader, as distinct from the administrator, bureaucrat, hierarch or boss, somehow sum up in their own personality and way of acting, something of the essence of the organisation they represent. This doesn't mean that they are perfect or invulnerable. In fact, like Saint Peter, they need to have experienced failure. At the time of his arrest Peter even went so far as to deny knowing Jesus and, under pressure, told a servant girl 'Woman I do not know him' (Luke 22:57). The result was that 'Because he was known in the early church community as a public sinner, he was a safe man to endow with leadership for he could never afford to take himself too seriously. If he ever degenerated into self-importance, people would only have to start talking about "cocks crowing" and Peter would have to laugh at himself – or die of embarrassment!'[13] The experience of human failure is often the beginning of wisdom.

A personality type that Benedict XVI himself has specifically singled out as unsuitable for episcopal appointment is the ambitious cleric. These are the priests who want to use the church as a career, and who aim to get as high as they can in the hierarchy. They are quite unsuited to any form of servant leadership. Speaking at an ordination ceremony in Saint Peter's on 7 May 2006 Benedict condemned 'careerism, the attempt to "get ahead", to gain a position through the church: to make use of and not to serve ... [The Careerist is] a man who wants to make himself important, to become a person of note through the priesthood; the image of someone who has as his aim his own exaltation and not the humble service of Jesus Christ.'[14] Most sensible priests these days would consider an episcopal appointment to be a poisoned chalice, especially within the context of the sexual abuse crisis when you never know what problems might be just around the corner in any diocese. But there seem to be some for whom ambition and ecclesiastical preferment is a motivating factor. Institutional power, leading ceremonies and wearing ecclesiastical regalia can clearly be something of an aphrodisiac.

But even if the church began to take the New Testament model of leadership seriously, and followed Benedict's advice about ambitious clerics, this would still not solve its leadership problems. By requiring celibacy as a prerequisite, the church simply sets itself an impossible task. As we have seen in the Introduction, this artificially limits the number of those who can serve in the priesthood and thus the episcopate. Benedict XVI may want to appoint better bishops, but he has a tiny, contracting pool of talent on which to draw if he limits himself to the present serving clergy. In a worldwide community of 1.098 billion Catholics the church draws its entire episcopate of 4600 bishops from a pool of 405 891 priests.[15] Despite the enormous leadership potential in the Catholic community the church artificially limits its choice to these men who have to be celibate, ordained at least 15 to 18 years and less than 65 years old. They also need at least a modicum of spirituality, intelligence and human talent and must be basically acceptable to the diocese to which they are appointed. They also should never have publicly disagreed with papal teaching, or said or done anything radical, or upset too many people, have no medical or psychological problems, not be in any type of intimate relationship that causes scandal, and have reasonable leadership skills, common sense and good judgment. It remains to be seen where Benedict is going to find enough suitable and talented men from such a restricted pool to lead Catholicism's almost 2900 dioceses and other ecclesiastical units. In other words the church is already in a situation in which its requirement of celibacy for the priesthood is seriously hindering its ministry and crippling the development of its leadership potential. This takes us back to the question of ordination, the priesthood and the role of laity in church leadership.

The reality is that many people provide leadership in the church: priests, religious, permanent deacons and laypeople. The role of priests increasingly has to be seen more broadly within the context of the renewal of the whole ministry of the church. Short-term solutions such as the importation of for-eign-born clergy, whether they are culturally sensitive or not, is simply not the solution. This stop-gap measure may well do more harm than good.

The only real answer is facing up to the question of the theology of ordained ministry and asking: who can be ordained? The shortage of clergy – and the creation of a much bigger pool of candidates for the episcopate – could be solved today. There is absolutely no theological or doctrinal reason why we cannot ordain suitably qualified married men. This has nothing to do with basic belief; it is merely a church law that can be changed today. If some coun-tries want to maintain celibacy – it is often claimed that India is an example – well, that's their business. Australia has quite specific pastoral and ministe-rial needs and it is our obligation to meet these needs. For some countries to have a married clergy will do no harm to the universal church. As a stop-gap measure there is also no reason why church law cannot be changed to allow priests in good standing who have left active ministry for whatever reason to volunteer to return to ministry after negotiation with the local bishop.

Many Catholics see a massive inconsistency and a lot of scandal in the fact that Catholicism has accepted convert married clergy into its ministry, par-ticularly from the Anglican and Lutheran churches in Germany, England, the USA, Canada, Australia and other countries, ordaining them often after only a cursory priestly, spiritual and theological formation while, at the same time refusing to accept the ministry of well-trained, theologically formed, minis-terially experienced Catholic priests who have left the active ministry usual-ly, but not always, to marry. It is also particularly galling when convert clergy from other churches indulge in commentary on celibacy. Early in 2005 the National Council of Priests (NCP) sent a series of reflections to the Australian bishops in preparation for the then forthcoming Synod on the Eucharist. They commented particularly on the shortage of priests 'and the consequent impossibility for many communities to celebrate the Eucharist frequently and regularly'. It was not right until the end of their comments that they asked that the Synod 'examine honestly the appropriateness of insisting upon a priesthood that is, with very few exceptions, obliged to be celibate. Priesthood is a gift; celibacy is a gift. They are not the same gift.' They also asked the bishops to consider the re-admission of priests who had left ministry for marriage.[16] Understandably this led to considerable comment in the media including statements by convert-Anglican, now married Catholic priest, John Fleming, extolling celibacy, but ignoring the ministerial deficit that Australian Catholicism is now facing through our acute shortage of priests. Celibacy, he said, was 'a witness to chastity in a fairly sexually-obsessed society, [it provides] greater portability, and it's cheaper to upkeep a celibate male than a family. There are huge implications for the life of the church, not least of which who is going to pay for married priests.'[17] It is significant that none of these reasons has anything to do with ministry and Eucharist, the context in which the NCP had framed the questions. Fleming seemed preoccupied with economic issues. A church that can find tens of millions of dollars for WYD can surely find the dollars needed to support a married clergy.

The fact is that celibacy is the symbol of a whole range of issues such as the role of laymen and women in ministry, authority in the diocese, parish and local community, and power and authority in the church. That is why the Vatican is so resistant to even discussing celibacy and is seemingly willing to sacrifice ministry to what is essentially a lifestyle issue. Most Catholics are sick to death of the spurious spiritual reasons advanced for the maintenance of celibacy. Recent crimes and scandals surrounding the clergy have given the lie to the notion that enforced celibacy leads to holiness or frees the priest for dedicated service. This is nothing more than a church law that has out-lived its usefulness.

The 2006 census shows the number of Australian Catholics increased by 125 260 or 2.5 per cent to 5 126 844 over the 2001 census. The number of active priests in 2007 was probably around 2150. That is one priest for around 2400 Catholics. This is much lower than in the US where the ratio is about one priest to 1900 Catholics. So while the number of Catholics continues to increase the number of priests continues to decrease and age. This is further complicated by the fact that the communities served are much more diverse and complex with greater demands placed on parochial leadership.

So what does this mean for parishes? Substantially it means that there are less and less priests available for pastoral work. This has resulted in the closing down or combining of parishes, or replacing priests with non-ordained pastoral associates (PAs). This is already happening in all Australian dioceses. A check through the Catholic Directory shows that two and sometimes three parishes are being combined under the care of one priest (so-called 'cluster parishes'). Other parishes are being left without personnel or placed under the care of a PA, or parishes are being closed altogether. Combining or closing a parish always involves the disturbance of an already established community. Closing down a parish is a painful and sometimes disastrous process.

The most positive scenario is the appointment of a non-ordained person to care for the parish. This is certainly better than the appointment of a foreign-born priest who might well be insensitive to cultural issues or have poor English skills (see Chapter 3). The appointment of PAs is already well established in Australia and will continue to increase. Here I am using the term 'pastoral associate' to cover all laypeople working professionally in ministry for which they receive a stipend or wage, as well as others working part-time or full-time, usually in sacramental and educational programs, voluntarily. The nomenclature used to describe these people is inconsistent and the Catholic Directory uses a variety of terms to cover PAs and certainly not all of those working in parishes are listed. Therefore it is very hard to be precise about exactly how many there are in Australia. A careful check of the Directory revealed that Australia-wide in 2007 there were *at least* 344 women (215 of these are religious sisters) and 31 men. Clearly these are the ones on a stipend, but there are many other unlisted people, both volunteers and paid workers.

The archdiocese of Melbourne lists the largest number of PAs by far, made up of 83 laywomen, 59 religious sisters and nine laymen. The situation is different in some dioceses where the large majority of all ministerial workers are religious sisters and there are no laypeople. In some cases, women PAs, usually sisters, are in charge of the parish. These Australia-wide figures are certainly minimal because 40 per cent of dioceses, for example Sydney and Cairns, only list priests even though I know there are PAs or their equivalents working in these dioceses. To the 375 PAs we need to add 33 laywomen (20 of whom are sisters) and 15 laymen who are listed as chaplains, working mainly in jails, universities and hospitals. Clearly without all of this lay ministerial help the Australian church's parochial ministry would collapse. In the United States this process is much more developed with some 31 000 PAs or 'lay ecclesial ministers'. About 80 per cent of these are women.[18]

Part of the difficulty in identifying PAs arises from the ambiguity that surrounds the use of the word 'ministry'. Despite the fact that almost everyone nowadays with some theological education talks about Christians having a 'ministry', church officials are wary about the word and usually only apply it to ordained ministry. Bishops, priests and deacons have a 'ministry'; the best laypeople can hope for is an 'apostolate'.

In Greek the word is *diakonia*, meaning both ministry and service. It is common in the New Testament. The problem is that within Catholicism since Vatican II the meaning of the word has been over-extended and the term itself overused. Listening to some people nowadays you would think that everybody in the church has a 'ministry', from the pope to the humblest member. What has happened is the word has been used as though everything that the Christian did, whether it was within the context of the church or not, was 'ministry'. In other words 'ministry' is evacuated of all meaning. Further confusion has arisen because in common parlance we have lost the distinction between discipleship and ministry. Every baptised person is a disciple of Jesus and has a general mission to serve others and proclaim their faith in the risen Christ, but that is not the same as being a minister. In the New Testament the word 'ministry' has a more specific meaning.

Australian theologian John N Collins in a detailed study has established the meaning of the term *diakonia* in the New Testament.[19] For Collins being a disciple is not the same as a minister, and he maintains that far too much emphasis has been placed on the notion of ministry as humble and lowly service to others. Part of the problem is that we read back into and impose upon the New Testament our contemporary interest in social welfare activities and care for the poorest. Collins says that being a minister in the New Testament's understanding meant that a person was called by God and the church to a public role in the proclamation of the gospel and celebration of the sacraments and that the role didn't necessarily imply a menial or lowly status. In fact it might even denote a person of significance, just as we use the word 'minister' today to denote someone of cabinet rank. In the early church people acting as ministers were not only officially appointed, but were subject to accountability and oversight. So when asked 'Are all Christians ministers?' Collins unequivocally answers 'No.'[20]

Some are critical of Collins' views on ministry because he clearly disagrees with the popular and widespread interpretation of ministry in progressive church parlance where everyone is a 'minister'. He limits the word to those individuals called to specific ministries. At first sight it seems that Collins is supportive of an almost hierarchical understanding of ministry in contrast to those at the more Protestant end of the spectrum who argue that baptism qualifies all Christians for ministry. Such an interpretation is to misunderstand Collins completely. Essentially he is arguing for a more exact use of the word to apply where the minister, whether man or woman, is called and commissioned by God through the church and the community to carry out a specific task which often has leadership or educational implications.

The context of ministry is always the church community. The minister is called to serve the community or to go out as a representative from it. It is the community that is basic and all Christian ministry is a service to it or an expression of it. The church is grounded in a community of equal disciples all of whom have the potentiality to be called to ministry. Ordination in the early church was specifically aligned to the community. That is a person was called and ordained to serve *this* community. That made sense in small urban communities in the late Roman world or in the early medieval world where travel was less common. To some extent this practise survives with diocesan priests tied through incardination to their diocese, but the problem is that theologically the emphasis nowadays is on that aspect of ordination which separates the ordained man from the community. It is seen as something 'absolute', something that ontologically changes the inner self of the ordinand. 'Once a priest, always a priest', as the saying goes.

Edward Schillebeeckx has shown that absolute ordination is contrary to the practise of the New Testament and the early church, which saw this sacrament as intimately related to the service of a particular community. This reveals the anomaly of moving priests around the world, usually from Africa and Asia to work in places where there is a so-called shortage of priests. As Schillebeeckx argues, there are always leaders and ministers already available, both men and women, but because of their blinkers about 'absolute' ordination and the requirement of celibacy the papacy and many of the bishops won't recognise them. Schillebeeckx doesn't mince matters: 'According to the views of the ancient church a shortage of priests was an ecclesiastical impossibility. The modern so-called shortage of priests therefore stands to be criticised in the light of the ancient church's view ... because the modern shortage has causes which stem from outside the ministry'; that is requirements like celibacy, seminary formation apart from the local community, and male gender issues.[21] The problem is not the Spirit of God who constantly raises up leaders for the local church, but obstacles falsely imposed by church law in the process of clericalising the ministry.

So what does all of this have to do with PAs? It means that the Holy Spirit has already provided leadership for the church which simply needs to be recognised, formed and commissioned. A PA in a parish has a specific and official task and this person is, in a proper theological sense, a minister and leader. PAs are not just lay replacements for the priest shortage, but Catholics with clear, specific and commissioned tasks. What are they actually doing? A whole range of things like liturgical preparation, catechesis both of primary and secondary students, as well as adult formation and Rite of Christian Initiation of Adults, counselling especially of bereaved people, communion and spiritual and material care of the sick, sacramental preparation, parish administration, faith formation and other roles. Certainly they need professional training and theological preparation for ministry. Perhaps a common national standard needs to be set for all working in pastoral ministry, with appropriate chances for specialisation, ultimately leading to a certificate or bachelor of pastoral care. A model for this is the system of clinical pastoral formation required by hospitals before someone can undertake chaplaincy with the sick. Ministry needs preparation and formation; this is not an attempt to 'professionalise' laypeople, but to prepare them to work effectively.

After completing a formation process there should be a liturgical installation, which focuses on the person's specific role in the ministry. For instance, if they are called to care for the sick, then they should be installed to administer those sacraments that are appropriate to that ministry which would at least include baptism and anointing. They can already bring communion. This claim is based on the theological principle that the sacraments are *propter homines*, in the service of people, and are under the control of the church. They are a means of sanctification, of putting people in contact with the transforming grace of God in Christ and there is no reason why they should be limited to seven, or that the nature of ordination not be extended. We could learn from the Eastern Orthodox tradition which has a far less strict definition of sacrament and doesn't limit them to seven.

Both the Eastern and Western churches have a tradition of sacramentals. These are liturgical actions and services, both public or private, such as blessings, holy water, ashes on Ash Wednesday, palms on Palm Sunday, lighting candles, touching statues and especially the Eastern tradition of using icons for prayer and liturgy. All of these practises are external signs of inward grace and of being touched by God. So perhaps we could begin by installing a PA through a standardised blessing ceremony with the status of a sacramental that symbolises the bestowal of the grace of the Holy Spirit to carry out their specific ministerial task. Then gradually the church might begin to recognise this as a form of ordination.

What all of this reveals is that lay ministry is one of those quiet revolutions that is going on right under our noses without a great deal of controversy. It is widely accepted in Australia even by some of the most cautious bishops. And Catholics in the pews have no problems with properly trained laypeople carrying out the various ministries of the church. Many of them rejoice in it. Rather than being a threat to priests, lay ministers actually highlight the real role of the priest: that is one of leadership, and bringing all the works of service into a focused unity, which is then celebrated in the Eucharist. Theologically there is a real sense in which the priest represents and actualises the function of the Holy Spirit in the local community. As the number of PAs grow Australian Catholicism will probably need less priests, probably just one in each parish. But to achieve this even now we will have to be willing to extend priestly ordination to a wider group of people. So while this important but quiet revolution doesn't excuse the church hierarchy from confronting the hard questions involved in the ordination of married men and of women, it does mean that something very positive is already happening in our parishes.

Australian Catholicism's other major ministry is education. Here the church has been forced by circumstances to show considerable creativity. One of the important changes that has already occurred is the fact that religious sisters and brothers have been almost totally replaced by lay teachers in Catholic schools, the majority of them laywomen. This transition from religious orders to laity is both a symptom and symbol of a profound and significant change in the socialising pattern of Australian Catholicism. The other influence is the increased involvement of governments in education and the granting of state aid to Catholic schools from the mid-1960s onwards.

Some historical perspective is important here. In the 1860s and 1870s the bishops faced an enormous challenge: to set up a primary school system from scratch. They achieved this because they were able to import teaching sisters, brothers and priests from Europe and especially Ireland. The fundamental issue was that the church was unwilling to allow secularism to dominate education. They contended that an explicitly Catholic ethos must permeate the whole of education. The bishops created, albeit unconsciously, a total socialising process whereby the church provided Australian Catholics with their primary community. They achieved this because they pressured working class Catholics into sending their children to Catholic schools where they were initiated into a whole religious and moral sub-culture. Not that all Catholics submitted, but the majority certainly did. The church was able to maintain this control until the early-1950s, ironically just before Catholics received state aid for their schools for which they had been agitating for so long.[22]

From the late-1960s onward the archdiocese of Melbourne was the leader among all Australian dioceses in the development of Catholic systemic schools. In an important study of this transition period between 1960 and 1980 Dr Anne O'Brien has shown that by 1963 'the Catholic education system in Victoria was on the verge of collapse'.[23] Post-war immigration and the 'baby boom' had led to a situation where standards in Catholic schools were plummeting and student–teacher ratios were untenable. I myself was in a class of over 80 boys at Christian Brothers College, Victoria Parade, East Melbourne in the first year of secondary in 1952, and O'Brien cites a sister in the late 1950s 'teaching 145 pupils in a partitioned hall, while the head teacher taught 112 pupils from three grades in the other half of the hall'.[24] By the mid-1960s the number of religious order teachers was dropping rapidly and the church had to find money not only for capital costs but also to pay an increasing salary bill for lay teachers. Because of shortage of space more and more Catholic children were forced to attend state schools; by 1974 this had reached 46 per cent. Both Labor and Liberal state governments were opposed to state aid to Catholic schools and so the future looked extremely bleak as the 1960s began. But change was already occurring at the federal level, especially after Prime Minister Robert Menzies nearly lost government in 1961.

In order for widespread change to occur it often takes a shock that makes people and politicians realise the consequences of a particular policy. That shock occurred in mid-1962. This was just eight years after the Labor split and the formation of the Democratic Labor Party (DLP). The church itself was divided between Melbourne's Archbishop Daniel Mannix and BA Santamaria's 'Movement', and Sydney's Cardinal Norman Gilroy and Archbishop James Carroll, who was very close to the right wing of the New South Wales Australian Labor Party (ALP). It was national ALP policy to oppose state aid to denominational schools and this was supported, if reluctantly, by Labor Catholics. The state aid issue came to a head on Monday, 16 July 1962 in Goulburn (which always had a high proportion of Catholics). The crisis resulted from the closing of all Catholic schools in Goulburn after the Health Department officiously demanded that three extra toilets be built at Our Lady of Mercy Preparatory School with a threat of fines and the withdrawal of accreditation. The Goulburn parishes and the Canberra archdiocese had no money to pay for the toilets and a group of parents seized the initiative supported by Auxiliary-Bishop John Cullinane, who was resident in Goulburn. At a public meeting parents and clergy decided to close all Catholic schools in Goulburn. As a result that Monday morning almost 1900 Catholic children arrived at local state schools and demanded admission. Only about a third of that number could be accommodated.

The impasse lasted a week and it received considerable media coverage. By the end of the week the point had been unmistakably made that the entire education system would collapse if Catholic schools were closed, and the New South Wales Heffron Labor government (Bob Heffron was a Catholic who had become a non-believer) was wrong-footed by the strike. They quickly paid for the toilet upgrade and initiated policy changes by beginning to offer help to build science laboratories in all schools including Catholic. But the state government was further embarrassed when the secularist-dominated national executive of the ALP overruled New South Wales and Heffron was forced to withdraw the offer. Prime Minister Menzies stepped in offering Commonwealth government grants for science education to be administered by the states. It was the beginning of a complex process that eventually led to increased federal funding for education with both major parties embracing state aid. One of the strongest proponents in the ALP was Gough Whitlam.[25]

In her book O'Brien describes the history of state aid and shows that Melbourne archdiocese led the way in making state aid a reality. This happened despite the divisive influence of the Santamaria movement on many bishops who, as O'Brien shows, were willing 'to sacrifice their schools for the sake of upholding the determination of the DLP/NCC [National Civic Council] to destroy the Labor Party'.[26] The chaos of the decades after the war was gradually organised into a Catholic school system that could responsibly deal with government, pay teachers' wages, decide where new schools should be built and how they would be paid for, and use taxpayer-funded aid in a way that complied with government regulations. The key figure in this process was Father Frank Martin, who had worked for many years in education and was director of the Melbourne Catholic Education Office (CEO) from 1970 onwards. Other dioceses gradually followed the Melbourne lead. It was the educational reforms of the Whitlam government between 1972 and 1975 and the establishment of the Schools Commission that finally gave education its due emphasis in national affairs and brought order and resources to both state and Catholic schools.

At the same time Vatican II and its aftermath was causing a revolution within the church. This led to a complete change in Catholicism's approach to teaching religion. Until the 1950s the central text for religious instruction was the 'penny catechism' (it actually cost six pence). It was a small book of questions and answers as well as prayers that students learned by heart. Religious formation consisted of a strong devotional and sacramental life with frequent school attendance at Mass and other services such as Benediction of the Blessed Sacrament, linked to a form of rote learning of prayers and formulae that were not geared to the development of the student and didn't particularly lend themselves to profound understanding.

However, as priest–historian Edmund Campion points out, things were already starting to change in the late 1950s with a whole new catechetical approach emerging in Europe.[27] The renewal was closely related to the liturgical movement and the centre of it was Germany. Theologians such as Joseph Jungmann, Johannes Hofinger, who visited Australia in the early 1960s, and

Francis H Drinkwater, developed a whole new approach to teaching religion with an emphasis on liturgy, biblical studies and the centrality of Jesus. There was also a strong link established with developmental psychology and students were taught material appropriate to their age. The new approach was reflected in two new *Catholic Catechisms*, one for upper primary and the other for lower secondary, with a teachers' book, which were published in 1962–63. They were largely the work of Monsignor John F Kelly of Melbourne.

The new catechisms were more Christocentric, with a strong emphasis on Jesus' role in the treatment of the sacraments, the church and the liturgy. They are rich in scriptural references and are geared to the developmental level of the student. The underlying theological approach focuses on God's love and forgiveness through Christ, replacing fear and guilt as motivating forces. Personal responsibility replaced obedience. Campion comments that the catechism was 'hailed internationally as the outstanding catechetical production of its day and appeared in overseas editions. The noticeable feature of Kelly's work was its dependence on the bible ... Teachers took to this new approach enthusiastically.'[28]

The period 1955 to 1975 saw an extraordinary change in Catholic education. Because of post-war immigration, Catholicism became multicultural long before the rest of Australia and Catholic schools reflected this. From the late 1960s onwards government money poured in resulting in the system expanding quickly with many new schools being built and with diocesan CEOs assuming more responsibility and authority. Lay teachers almost entirely replaced religious and the old system which was the church's 'main socialising agency disappeared ... quickly without anyone, bishops, priests or people being prepared for the changes or having any clear idea about what to do next'.[29] The result was a period of confusion. Unfortunately Kelly's catechisms quickly fell into disuse especially in secondary schools; perhaps the mistake was that an upper secondary text was never produced. Part of the problem was also that textbooks were no longer popular and so-called 'creativity' was all the rage in education. Significant mistakes were made. This is especially true of the *Kum By Ya* period in the 1970s and 1980s when many schools abandoned theological and intellectual content in religious education and replaced it with feelings and emotions and 'finding your own way'. This resulted in widespread religious ignorance, especially for Generation X.

What has been the impact of this on religious formation in Catholic schools? Fortunately the late Brother Marcellin Flynn interviewed and surveyed almost 6000 year 12 students as well as teachers in Catholic schools from 1972 until 1998. The results were published in two books, *The Culture of Catholic Schools* and *Catholic Schools – 2000*.[30] The latter book has the most interesting comparative information because it looks across a longitudinal perspective over four surveys taken in 1972, 1982, 1990 and 1998.

Some of the more significant findings are that the example and lives of parents are the most important influence on year 12 students' religious development with 71 per cent rating this as important, as against 54 per cent nominating friends and peers, 36 per cent a school retreat or camp, 24 per cent the schools' religious education program and 23 per cent school Masses and liturgies. Flynn concludes that

> parental influence, together with the influence of the Catholic school
> appear largely to determine whether they grow up Christian and Catholic
> ... Practising Catholic students tend to come from more religious families
> where their faith has been nurtured and developed by the lives of their
> parents.

Because friends are also important, practising students in turn influence others. Certainly religious education and school retreats and liturgies have an important role to play, but the influence of the parish is negligible.[31]

There has been a collapse in students' attendance at Sunday Mass from 69 per cent in 1972 to 23 per cent in 1998, a drop of 46 per cent.[32] The practise of the sacrament of confession or reconciliation has also dramatically declined from 35 per cent of year 12s attending more than or at least once a month in 1972 to 3 per cent in 1998.[33] On core belief issues such as God and Christ there is a consistently strong belief in God and God's loving fatherhood. Belief in God's forgiveness also remains strong as does an experience of God's closeness. There is a significant increase in the number of year 12s who say that 'Christ is a real person to me in my daily life'. Fifty-one per cent believe Jesus Christ is truly God and truly present in the Eucharist, but oddly in 1998 only 33 per cent believed Jesus was 'truly man', down from 57 per cent in 1982. In 1998 40 per cent said they spent time in prayer each day and 37 per cent said they based their lives on 'the teaching and example of Christ'. Fifty-one per cent said that 'knowing Jesus helps me to be a better person'.[34]

Nevertheless, year 12 students in 1998 had quite a negative attitude to Religious Education (RE). Half of them said that RE doesn't interest them and 39 per cent complained that it took up too much time. Flynn believes these responses 'are a matter of some concern. There are strong suggestions that the growing secular culture of Australian society is tending to marginalise the religious dimension of Catholic schools for which the schools were originally founded'. He reports that in their qualitative responses year 12 students reflected 'a certain anger'. This is an understatement in light of some of the responses he quotes. Here are two typical comments: 'I dislike it [RE] immensely! I believe it should be voluntary. I find it has no relevance to my life, my faith or what I believe or wish to believe. It gets in the way of our difficult, more time-consuming subjects I don't want *have to learn* RE at school!' Then there's this: 'I think years 11 and 12 [RE] is a complete waste of time. It serves no purpose in my opinion, other than adding to my already heavy workload. Religious education classes have no bearing or importance in my life after leaving school and so I see absolutely no point in them.'[35]

Schools should not be fazed by such comments and Flynn reports that there has been an increasingly strong emphasis, particularly at the upper levels of secondary, on assessment of students' knowledge and understanding of RE in recent years. Another positive move has been the use of retreats for year 12 students, although the 1998 survey shows a sharp decline in the positive response to retreats.[36] Parents often say they send their children to Catholic schools because of the discipline. This is certainly borne out in year

12 students' responses concerning school discipline which Flynn says has 'improved significantly over the past three decades'.[37]

What does this tell us? Firstly, Catholic schools have been transformed in the 35 years since Vatican II. As Graham English has pointed out, the emphasis on the love of God and the dissipation of fear as a motive for religious practise and moral behaviour, have changed attitudes radically. Catholics now rely more on conscience than authority to make decisions about moral issues, especially those surrounding gender and sexuality. Schools are no longer the 'primary socialising agency' but have become 'places of evangelisation, social justice, a sacramental approach to life, and a way of introducing children to a Catholic way of being. Religious education [takes] scripture and theology more seriously and devotion [has] become less prominent.'[38] English makes the point that parents now want 'pastoral care, discipline [and] good quality education'. RE is low on their list of priorities. What Catholic schools really do is evangelise by giving their students a chance to experience what the broader Catholic community is like, and model the ideals that Catholicism tries to live. He says that attempts to resurrect 'an obedient, devout, uniform Catholic community' in the style of the 1950s is impossible because we live in a different world in which ways of socialising the younger generation have completely changed.

Flynn comes to the same conclusion. He points out that the contemporary church attracts educated and theologically sophisticated teachers who are 'highly professional ... [and] respected for their teaching competence and for the pastoral care they show towards students'. Flynn says that it is the principal who 'sets the tone and quality of a school's culture in quite explicit ways'.[39] The principal must act as a community leader who provides religious, pastoral and educational inspiration. To be pastoral leaders principals must model in their own lives the Catholic ethos, beliefs and values for which the school stands.

At Canberra's MacKillop Catholic College the *Senior School Handbook* is unequivocal. It says the school 'is a Catholic educational institution. As such, it strives to provide an education which is distinctively Catholic and based on gospel values ... The Religious Education programs will give students opportunities to pray, to worship and celebrate the sacraments. All students will be encouraged to extend their knowledge, understanding and appreciation of their Catholic heritage as well as their knowledge and understanding of other faiths.'[40] It is precisely this kind of approach to RE which emphasises Catholicism and its heritage, but that is at the same time respectful of other faiths, that is best suited to the educational and ministerial needs of our time. While comparative religion should not be neglected, my emphasis would be on Catholicism. Experienced RE teachers at MacKillop told me that in the 1970s and 1980s the level of interest in RE was low and student attitudes antagonistic, but that nowadays this has changed. There is considerable interest among the brightest students in higher tertiary-level classes in religious studies, and they find that this interest increases with academic rigour.

Unfortunately it is also clear that some Catholic schools still treat RE as a low status subject. This is shown by schools that regularly drop RE classes for another subject or purpose. Another problem is that individual schools and RE teachers have a fair degree of latitude in deciding how courses develop within the general framework set by the various CEOs. Much depends on what teachers are actually trying to achieve in RE, what purpose they have in mind, and how they conceive their role.

There are several options. Some want to return to a catechising approach, to teach students 'The Truth' through a kind of watered-down, old-style theology so that they emerge from school 'knowing what the church teaches', as well as having a clear awareness of what the pope and Vatican teach on morals and the rules and regulations governing Catholic behaviour. This is essentially a return to the pre-1960s, with the clear expectation that this whole complexus will somehow socialise students into the faith. At the other end of the spectrum is an emphasis on a kind of generic religio-spiritual formation so that students emerge understanding how faith and spirituality work across a range of cultures and religious traditions, including their own, resulting in a kind of mish-mash approach in which – although it is never said in so many words – one religion is as good as another. They are more likely to say that 'they are all different ways to the same God'. At best this approach gives students a kind of religious literacy, at worst it leaves them with a confusing array of half-understood religious 'choices'.

Somewhere between these two is what I think is the right approach for a Catholic school. This involves setting out to educate students about Catholic Christianity and ultimately to form and involve them in some level of commitment to faith in Christ. This is achieved not just through RE, but involves the whole staff in taking religion, faith and spirituality seriously and professionally, and reflecting in their relationships with students at least a basic Christian level of pastoral care and sensitivity. For senior people in the school such as the principal, vice-principal and RE co-ordinator, as well as RE teachers, this involves a serious and integral commitment to Catholicism, its faith tradition, spirituality and morality, as well as a basic professional knowledge of its theology. Catholic education claims to be offering something different to other schools, and this difference is essentially expressed in living within the ambit of Catholicism expressed through its faith, worship, spirituality, pastoral care, ministry, culture and history. The school as a whole needs to be able to reflect something of all of these commitments and values, and if they are not present the school is Catholic in name only.

It is true that genuine Catholic education makes very big demands on the core staff and particularly the RE teachers. This is especially so because Catholic schools are probably the only contact many students have with Catholicism. As Niola Curtis points out, school offers 'the only comfortable opportunity to engage in critical reflection and discussion about religion and their church'.[41] Given the failure of many parents to pass on the faith, this educational experience is important because faith involves a life-long process and the Catholic school may well be the only foundation upon which a genuinely spiritual and committed life can be built later. Curtis also says that teaching RE is very hard work and getting the services of committed, competent RE teachers is difficult. Many are forced to teach the subject to get promotion in the Catholic system, even though they have no interest in religion. Others are not Catholic, some not even Christian and they have real problems dealing with a tradition that is not their own.

Others, for various reasons related to their own faith-journey, are struggling to maintain their commitment to Catholicism. They may be troubled by guilt or depression, or facing problems with divorce and remarriage, family break-up, gender identity, a feeling of a loss of faith or, more likely, a loss of confidence in the church. This can make teaching RE very difficult. Curtis comments that

> If teachers do not have confidence and indeed trust in themselves and what they are doing it is difficult, if not impossible, to provide students with opportunities to speak out, to develop critical thinking practises and feel 'OK' about debating, discussion and even contradicting current and past church practise and beliefs.

But, at the same time, it needs to be remembered that genuine faith and belief is tested and everyone, even the most committed, go through periods of aridity and personal and interpersonal crisis.

This doesn't necessarily say someone should get out of RE teaching because they are experiencing doubt. Perhaps it just indicates that they need some form of pastoral support or just a chance to talk things over with someone sensible. A possible answer to this might be to adapt executive coaching, which often helps senior managers administer complex organisations. It is conceivable that schools might have a kind of 'spiritual coach', a mature and experienced person from outside the school with whom RE teachers can talk through issues, both personal and professional. You would only need one person for a number of schools. While the RE co-ordinator can be helpful, it is sometimes better to speak to someone from outside who is not a colleague and who is thus less threatening and more objective.

The church needs RE teachers who are ministerially confident, critical and reflective and who are able to grow through their own faith crises and use them to assist and understand their students. Catholic schools have got to be willing to sink more resources into RE, to make sure committed teachers are respected as specialists and are given ample opportunities for ongoing in-service training and tertiary education and perhaps to pay them a premium over-and-above their normal professional award. Catholic schools have got to show that they treat RE not only as a core subject, but as the central reason why the school exists.

The Australian church's school system has few overseas parallels and is a major component in the church's ministry. On 8 August 2007, the bishops of New South Wales and the Australian Capital Territory issued a Pastoral Letter entitled *Catholic Schools at a Crossroads* warning that current trends in Catholic education have brought them to a point of re-assessment. Largely written by Bishop Anthony Fisher, auxiliary bishop of Sydney, the Pastoral called on Catholics to dedicate themselves to ensuring four goals: first, that schools are 'truly Catholic in their identity and life'; second, that they are centres of 'the new evangelisation'; third, that schools enable students 'to achieve high levels of "Catholic religious identity"'; fourth, that they 'are led and staffed by people who will contribute to these goals'. The Pastoral points out that many poor Catholic families cannot afford to send children to Catholic schools with half of all Catholic students enrolled in state schools. Also an increasing proportion of students from wealthier families are going to non-Catholic independent schools. In other words Catholic schools are serving middle Australia rather than the poor. The Pastoral warns that students often 'have little or no connection with the Church outside their school'. Also up to 40 per cent of students are from non-Catholic families. The result is that the schools 'now have a different mix of students and less support for their specifically religious mission from outside the school than they had in the past. The surrounding culture and its powerful agents such as the media and new technologies are also commonly less supportive'. In a clear reference to weak theology and poor catechesis the Pastoral admits that 'not all of our students have been as well served catechetically or pastorally as they might have been' by Catholic schools.[42] We have already seen in this book that 'fewer young people now identify themselves with churches or religions' and the Pastoral warns that 'Society-wide trends such as secularisation, consumerism, family dysfunction and values disorientation also impact upon young people'.[43] These issues effect not only Catholic education, but other ministries.

Nevertheless, the Australian Catholic church has a unique ministerial opportunity in its school system. It exists to a considerable extent outside clerical control, essentially because it has its own structures, is staffed by laity and is funded by government. Pastoral Letters notwithstanding, even the most intrusive bishop would have difficulty exercising any real influence over it. The key issue is that this is a lay ministry involving large numbers of Catholics. Most are committed to an essentially evangelical vision, that gives students an experience of the symbolic, imaginative and spiritual, that teaches them to think broadly and critically about issues that touch on the philosophical, but that above all gives them an experience of faith, love and community that is not fundamentalist. If they leave school with at least some inkling of the genius of Catholicism, the school will have done its work. What lies ahead of them is a whole lifetime during which they can develop the faith-experience and insight that the Catholic school gave them.

6

Does Australian Catholicism have a future?

Does Australian Catholicism have a future? Could it slowly degenerate into an empty shell lacking hope and a sense of ministry, and become just another entity offering government-funded services? Is there a danger of the passion disappearing as the Catholic community loses its essential commitment to the person and message of Jesus? Looking at the evidence in Chapters 1 and 2 these might seem like unnecessary questions. The extraordinary ministerial structure of the Australian Catholic church, much of it funded by government, seems to be doing remarkably well. And, as we saw, sociologists like Gary Bouma think Catholicism is far from imminent collapse in Australia.

However, these are not just speculative questions. Historically Catholicism has lost constituencies before in specific places with a widespread abandonment of the faith. This usually happens not so much by outright attack or persecution, as by a failure of leadership in the church and the seduction of the Catholic community by the prevailing cultural ethos. For example, take contemporary Catholicism in the Republic of Ireland. The church has dominated Irish culture and the state since independence from the UK in 1920. For decades Ireland was a major exporter of clergy to other countries, including Australia. Catholicism is now in major crisis with a widespread collapse in commitment among young people and only eight priestly ordinations for the whole of Ireland in 2005. The rot has set in so badly that Archbishop Diarmuid Martin of Dublin gave a lecture in July 2005 entitled 'Will Ireland be Christian in 2030?' Despite the fact that the church remains a major force in Irish primary and secondary education, it is not holding on to young adults who are abandoning Catholic belief in droves to live a purely secular life. Clearly the church has a major credibility problem resulting from its public insistence on strict sexual morality for the laity, while secretly covering-up widespread priestly misconduct and child sexual abuse among the clergy. This warns us that a self-satisfied, arrogant church with poor episcopal leadership could be sitting on a powder-keg.

The tendency on the part of many church leaders and more conservative Catholics is to blame forces outside Catholicism for the church's failures, such as 'secularisation, consumerism, family dysfunction and values disorientation' as the New South Wales bishops put it in their Pastoral on Catholic schools. The argument is that our culture is suffering from a lack of spirituality and a crisis of faith in Christ. But this is actually putting the cart before the horse. The primary responsibility for the church's pastoral failures lies squarely within its own structures and with its own leadership. As I said in the Introduction: the church is its own worst enemy. It deludes itself that external social forces or an internal 'faith collapse' are to blame when the primary cause lies within itself. This is not to claim that external forces are not important. Contemporary post-modern society is not an easy context in which to live the spiritual life of a committed believer. But the primary stumbling blocks to a creative approach to ministry and pastoral care in Australia today lie within the church itself.[1]

The greatest threat to the church comes from the lack of creative leadership at a diocesan and national level, as well as from the failure of the papacy to acknowledge the ministerial crisis facing local churches like Australia. In this and a number of previous books I have been critical of the papal ministry of John Paul II precisely because he consistently refused to confront the internal issues facing Catholicism. While recognising his accomplishments, it has to be admitted that his internal leadership of the church, especially in the area of ministry, was disastrous. All of the ministerial issues that most trouble Catholics, such as the shortage of priests, the denial of the Eucharist and sacraments to millions of Catholics and the ministerial role of women, were simply ignored or stymied for 27 years. Despite my initial optimism that Benedict XVI might come to grips with some of these issues, I now feel that there is little evidence that he will take action. I am now convinced that change will not come from the top. Another 'John XXIII' or a 'progressive pope' who will act as a kind of circuit-breaker or messiah for reform-minded Catholics is a most unlikely possibility.

That is why bishops are so important. But a central problem is that many bishops feel that their sole line of responsibility is upward to Rome, because it was the Vatican that appointed them. There is little or no consciousness that they have responsibility to the local church and that they must answer to priests and laity. Vatican domination is re-enforced by the fact that the few Australian bishops who have shown courageous leadership have been quickly subjected to investigation and censure by the Vatican. This creates the notion that bishops are branch managers and enforcers of the policies of head office. This is a complete distortion of traditional Catholic doctrine and this view really only became widespread in the 19th and 20th centuries when almost all episcopal appointments were taken over by the Vatican. This is one of a number of distortions that have resulted from the over-centralisation of the church that has occurred over the last two centuries. While Vatican II theoretically restored the episcopate to its traditional place in the church, John Paul II maintained the distortion by appointing many papal 'yes men' lacking vision and leadership ability as bishops.

In June 2007 I was part of a group who wrote to every bishop in Australia. We asked them to consider the fact that there was already a major crisis of ministry and leadership in Australian Catholicism. We believed that this was crippling the church's capacity to provide Mass and the sacraments for the Catholic community. The priest shortage was also damaging the church's ability to provide pastoral care and was limiting its missionary role in the wider secular community. We conceded that bishops were constrained in what they can do by the Vatican, but pointed out that the Catholic tradition is clear: the bishop's primary responsibility is to his diocese and more broadly to the national church. So we asked each bishop individually and the bishops as a conference to acknowledge that there is a major crisis in ministry within the Australian Catholic church and to admit that there is no doctrinal or theological barrier to the ordination of married men. We pointed out that the Australian church has already ordained former Anglican priests and allows marriage among Eastern Rite clergy in union with Rome. We asked them to take practical steps toward ordaining suitably qualified and trained married men, as well encouraging wide-ranging discussion on the role of women in ministry and in the authority structures of the church, including the question of women's ordination. We called for appropriate scriptural, theological and pastoral training programs to prepare suitable people for ministry. These candidates should have the recommendation of their parishes and communities. Finally to bridge the time-gap between the gradual introduction of married clergy we asked the bishops to invite priests who had left the ministry to return to active priesthood, subject to negotiation with the local diocese. We also pointed out that there are already many people in our communities who are well educated in theology and liturgy and are gifted with talent for pastoral ministry and leadership.

The petition received a real fillip when Canberra Auxiliary Bishop Patrick Power came out publicly in support. He noted that 'At the heart of the issue is the relationship of the local church to the universal church ... for a number of years (some would say since the beginning of John Paul II's pontificate) there has been a greater encroachment on the life of the local church which has given the diocesan bishop and his collaborators little scope for effective leadership.' Power was not alone. A week after he had gone public, retired Bishop Geoffrey Robinson published his book *Confronting Power and Sex in the Church*.[2] Using his personal journey and the sexual abuse crisis as a prism, Robinson examined Catholic morality, spirituality and the authority structure of the church. The book said little that was new, but it certainly focused the issues about which many of us had been speaking for decades. The media gave it widespread coverage because Robinson is a bishop. My own feeling at the time was that rather than endlessly talking about the issues, I wanted Robinson or any bishop to *do* something, like ordaining some married men or women, either married or single, or at least returning a married priest to pastoral service. If you are going to get into trouble with Rome it ought to be for something worthwhile! The time for talking is over and the time for action has arrived.

While highlighting the ministerial issues that must be addressed urgently, at the core of what we were trying to do was to get the bishops to acknowledge that they not only had to answer to Rome for their episcopal ministry, but also to the local church. In traditional theology, bishops are successors of the apostles in their own right; as such they are not dependent on Rome for their ministerial authority. Acting together in a college with the pope they are also responsible for the government of the universal church. But more importantly they have a primary line of responsibility to their local church. Their essential vocation is to lead the diocesan community and their primary responsibility is to it, and more broadly to the national church represented in Australia by the ACBC. But it is very hard to get most bishops to acknowledge this. Those without great leadership ability tend always to want to please their 'superiors' in Rome. They feel their primary line of responsibility is to the Vatican and they treat the local community as completely subordinate to this priority. More able, ambitious bishops also look to Rome as their point of reference. They are on a career path and their central aim is to please the patrons who will ensure their promotion. Both groups of bishops treat the local church as secondary and repress any view that remotely contradicts the Roman line.

Fortunately, Australia still has a majority of bishops whose orientation is essentially pastoral, and whose primary care is for their dioceses. Father Eric Hodgens has analysed the Bishops' Conference and he divides it into three loose groupings. I would call these groups 'the boots-and-all brigade', 'the time-servers', and 'the pastoralists'. Hodgens describes the first group as 'hard right wing and fundamentalist'. However, there are no more than six of them. The time-servers 'support the Roman line for ideological or opportunistic reasons'. My count would be that there are between seven and 10 of these, almost all in powerful positions. The rest fit into the pastoral category. There are 43 active bishops; this means that about 27 fit into the pastoral category. Hodgens argued in July 2006 'Now is the time for them to caucus, get a leader and act – redeem the situation. And they must do it urgently ... Their successors will simply not have the nous. Now is our last chance.'[3] He is right.

What does all of this tell us? Essentially it means that the process of appointing bishops has to be changed. In place of the complex Roman system, which is geared to eliminating creative leadership and to the appointment of papal 'yes men', we need to recover the traditional system of selecting bishops. Certainly this evolved over the centuries, but the emphasis was always on the local church. The first method was by direct election of the whole community. Over the centuries the franchise became increasingly constricted, mainly because of the politics involved, and it gradually became limited to the senior priests of a diocese. This practise still survives in a couple of dioceses in Austria and Switzerland where the canons of the cathedral draw up the *terna*, the list of three names to be sent to Rome. Also for the first 900 years of church history, bishops could not transfer from diocese to diocese. Once elected they were there for life, 'married' to their diocese. The purpose was to preclude ambitious clerics from using smaller dioceses as stepping-stones to more prestigious appointments. But this prohibition began to break down in the 9th century and bishops became mobile, although much less so than in the last 100 years. However, as a general rule all appointments before the 19th century originated in the local area.[4] The process was that 'bishops were elected locally, approved by their metropolitan [the senior regional arch-bishop], and acted largely independently of Rome. In other words the church was decentralised and the principle of subsidiarity was respected.'[5] Certainly, after the late-Middle Ages, bishops of important dioceses were usually chosen by the local king or ruler in consultation with the papacy and other interested parties, although in many places the canons of the cathedral still played an important role in episcopal appointments. The practise of Rome appointing all bishops is very recent and goes back to the mid-19th century.

Today we need to recover the process whereby local priests, ministers and laity can play a real role in episcopal appointments. In pluralist, democratic societies like Australia, people are used to voting responsibly and peacefully, in sharp contrast to people in the past who had no experience of democracy; this often led to violence on the part of those who lost an episcopal election. Perhaps the best system would be for an elected representative diocesan synod of clergy, laity and members of religious orders to suggest three names in order of preference, with the ACBC usually approving the first nomination. The Vatican would not participate in the process unless there were disputes. This is not a revolution, but a return to the more traditional process used by Catholicism to elect its leadership for a millennium or more. The Australian Anglican church manages to elect its diocesan bishops at synods at least semi-democratically without too much ado. Certainly there will be politics involved, but given our democratic background and experience Australian Catholics should be able to weather this process.

But this also requires that the pool of people who could be nominated as bishops needs to be expanded from the ordained and incardinated priests of a particular diocese. The great 4th-century bishop, Saint Ambrose, was a Roman secular administrator and lawyer and, although a believer, he was not even a baptised Catholic when he was elected bishop of Milan in 374. He had to do a crash course in theology to get up to speed! He became one of the greatest preachers of the age and was influential in the conversion of Saint Augustine. The election of laymen as bishops was relatively common in the first seven centuries of church history. Clearly the election of a layperson as bishop would be closely linked with the acceptance of married men into the priesthood. These are actually not big changes; it's just hard to imagine them, because we have become so cowed by the present system, forgetting that there have always been other options. In all of this the role and leadership of women must be carefully considered, because they carry out 75 per cent of the pastoral work of the Australian church.

None of this will be achieved from the top down, but can only be brought about from the bottom upwards. Those at the top of the hierarchy in the Vatican, even if they are saints, have too much invested in the maintenance of the structure to perceive the need for the kind of renewal required. This is why the fidelity of a group of serious and committed Catholics at the core of the church is so important. It is their passionate adherence to a renewed vision of Catholicism, no matter what the obstacles, that will be the essential element in realising a whole new way of envisaging and living the faith. This connects closely with a second element in what has happened to Catholics, especially in the long papacy of John Paul II. This pope turned the church into a one man band and did great harm by focusing attention on himself and on what the Vatican allowed or didn't, thus completely undermining the principle of subsidiarity (that decisions be taken at the lowest level possible rather the top) and rendering other ministries secondary and irrelevant. Everything came back to the pope; he was Catholicism incorporated, take it or leave it. This is a complete distortion of traditional church government. As a result the church's active ministry lost many people, including large numbers of priests and laypeople, who could have shown real leadership in dioceses and parishes. Essentially what happened was that they lost hope. They are the people who in the words of novelist Morris West have experienced 'the deep hurt and division … within the post-Vatican II generation, who … see the fading of the hopes they had invested in the updating and renewal of the church'.[6]

Catholicism needs be re-energised with the passion of hope. Our world is characterised by anxiety and a search for security, not only personal and financial, but also immunity against the external threats posed by fundamentalist fanaticism. Yet, ironically, one of the focal sources of modern angst is the attempt to live without any sense of God or the transcendent, without faith in anything. This has become particularly virulent with the recent publication of Richard Dawkins and Christopher Hitchens' tomes attacking all forms of religious belief and equating mainstream faith with fundamentalism. These authors actively oppose God and set out to explain reality as the product of evolution, without any sense of transcendence or spirituality. In the process they cut off any possibility of hope and creativity for a better world. Modern anxiety constitutes one of the basic ministerial challenges for Catholicism: to offer a sense of hope and trust in God to the wider world.

But the church also seems trapped in its own foreboding. Among Catholics, both active and inactive, there is a kind of depression, a feeling that no matter what the layperson or the local priest does, nothing will happen, because the levers of power are firmly in the hands of those who want to re-interpret Vatican II out of existence. However, if we could achieve some of the ministerial issues that I have outlined, or there was a broadening of ordination, or there was some movement around the issue of the election of bishops, then a sense of hope could be recovered. It would be a motivation for many to return to the church. Reconciling disaffected groups is precisely one of the reasons why Benedict XVI says he has encouraged the restoration of the 16th century Latin liturgy of the Council of Trent. He says that 'in some regions no small numbers of faithful adhered and continued to adhere with great love and affection to the earlier liturgical forms. These had deeply marked their culture and spirit.' So, following their 'insistent prayers', in July 2007, he gave permission to celebrate the Tridentine Latin liturgy.[7] What is interesting is that he acted against the advice of the majority of the world's bishops because, he claimed, he was so pastorally concerned for what we have already seen is a minuscule group of people.

In the light of this, the question occurs: what about the enormous number of other Catholics who are also disaffected because, despite their 'great love and affection' for the Mass and sacraments, they have been deprived of these core celebrations because of the shortage of priests? These are the same people who committed themselves and generously embraced the reforms of Vatican II when asked by the church. So what is Benedict going to do for them? When will he provide them with enough priests to celebrate the Eucharist?

So those Catholics really concerned about the church's ministry will need to hang on firmly to the virtue of hope, because it is this alone that will sustain them through the hard work of changing the church from the bottom up, given the complete failure of pastoral leadership at the top levels in contemporary Catholicism. It is also the only way to be true to Jesus who died a seeming failure on the cross. Saint Paul takes Abraham as his model of hope. He says that Abraham 'hoping against hope ... believed that he would become "the father of many nations" ... He did not weaken in his faith when he considered his own body, which was already as good as dead (for he was about 100 years old), or when he considered the barrenness of Sarah's womb. No distrust made him waiver concerning the promise of God' (Romans 4:18–20). Hope is very much at the core of Pauline theology and cosmology. In the Letter to the Romans (8:19–30) he develops the extraordinary image of the cosmos and humanity passing through a process of giving birth to a new world as we wait 'for our bodies to be set free'. He sees this as a process that is as old as the universe itself and at the essence of it is a hope-filled dynamism in which all of us play our part. 'Our salvation is not in sight, we should not have to be hoping for it if it were ... we must hope to be saved since we are not saved yet – it is something we must wait for with patience' (Romans 8:24–25).[8] For Paul, hope is the dynamism that drives the whole of creation, the reality that brings us liberation when 'our bodies are set free' from the anxiety that cripples us and turns us into cynics.

At the core of Catholicism's ministry is the proclamation of this radical sense of trust. This is not a mere velleity, an optimistic hankering that things will somehow come good. It is a belief that, if people are committed, change and liberation can occur. It is a dynamic belief that what God wants will be achieved if we work hard to carry out what we discern to be God's will. It won't be exactly what we think should happen, but God's Spirit writes straight with our crooked lines to protect the Eucharistic and sacramental life of Catholicism, church leadership notwithstanding. A renewal of ministry will bring life to the church and create the circumstances in which a new evangelisation can occur. The 14th century English mystic and anchoress, Dame Julian of Norwich (circa 1342–1416), writing in the period of despair just after the Black Death, wondered why God permitted sin and hell. Jesus answered her enigmatically, but with a profound sense of hope:

> I make all things well, and I can make all things well, and I shall make all
> things well, and I will make all things well; and you will see for yourself
> that every kind of thing will be well ... And in these words God wishes us
> to be enclosed in rest and peace.[9]

According to John Paul II in his 2001 Apostolic Exhortation *Ecclesia in Oceania* addressed to the peoples of Australia and the Pacific, nurturing a sense of hope is a key element in the 'new evangelisation', and the New South Wales bishops say this is one of their key priorities in their Pastoral Letter on Catholic schools. They say that evangelisation 'is all the more urgent in the context of the growing numbers of non-practising Catholics, under-catechised Catholics and other-than-Catholic students in our schools.' The Pastoral sets out a basic program through which evangelisation might be achieved.[10] While understandably the bishops want to present a practical way through which this goal can be achieved in the school context, I suspect they are jumping the gun. A lot of people talk about 'evangelisation', but what is almost always lacking is a developmental, psychological and coherent theological approach to how this process is carried out. All ministry is a form of evangelisation, and involves a multi-layered approach that takes seriously the background and level of faith commitment of the person or group being addressed. In any school different students will be at different places regarding belief and will range from those with no faith to those who are seriously committed. People at different places on the faith-spectrum will require different approaches.

As a way of making sense of evangelisation, I have set it out as a three-pronged process: pre-evangelisation, evangelisation, and catechesis, which aims at developing and deepening the faith of those who are already believers. Here, I think, is a basic agenda for the future of the Australian church.[11]

Firstly, what is pre-evangelisation? It is essentially the creation of an atmosphere that says that faith and belief should be taken seriously, that God and spirituality are realities in human life and that assists in spreading human and Christian ideals and values. This is where hope enters the picture. Catholicism should reflect a hope-filled community that ultimately trusts life, that draws people out of their self-obsessed subjectivity and is dedicated to a sense that every event in our individual and communal lives has meaning and that life has a direction and purpose. Another way of looking at it is the re-enforcement of the conviction that religion and spirituality ought to be taken seriously. Through many years working professionally in the secular media and commenting on religious issues, I have become convinced that all I have ever done is a form of pre-evangelisation. My underlying agenda has been that religion is worth talking about and it is just as important in public discourse as politics, economics, foreign affairs, public policy, health and the other things the media takes seriously. In faith terms, what I have been doing is preparing the ground, awakening a sense of the possibility of access to the transcendent and the spiritual. I always resisted the 'bible-bangers' who called in to talk-back radio shows to quote scriptural texts on the supposition that if listeners heard the Word there was a chance that they would be smitten and converted. It is no use plunging people into the bible or doctrine without preparation or respect for their religious development. You have to take people where they are.

Essentially, pre-evangelisation is shown in the Christ-like attitude of those ministering. This will be difficult if people are employed by the church *solely* on the basis of their professionalism without any consideration of their ability to mirror the kind of hope, compassion, justice, decency, sympathy, openness and the other traits characteristic of Christian faith. The ministry of the church is based on the presupposition that it is specifically Christian. A Catholic hospital, or school, or aged-care facility, or charity is not any secular or government agency. This is not to denigrate what others do in these areas. It is simply to say that the specific difference of a Catholic institution is that the people working in it reflect the person and message of Jesus. While they probably won't articulate this, people expect that in Catholic institutions they will be treated with the kind of dignity, integrity and goodness with which God treats them.

The problem is Catholicism has a long way to go to recover the sense that it reflects the integrity of God and the gentleness of Christ. The sexual abuse crisis has done enormous harm, but it is not only that. The kind of uncompromising, unfriendly and unattractive 'boots and all', bully-boy style of Catholicism that is often reflected by some leading church people probably does even more harm. Sadly, so many of the webpages and discussion boards on the net that claim to represent or reflect on Catholicism are run by aggressive, reactionary Catholics. Some of them are astonishingly rude and arrogant, and much of the discussion is carried on in the most extraordinarily vicious and confronting terms. Although these comments are a reflection on one particular Australian discussion board, they can be applied fairly broadly: 'Vituperation, name-calling, shrill denunciation, sneering and an entirely unconvincing triumphalism are the principal modes of expressing disagreement on any issue.' Often these boards and webpages 'present the most unappealing possible picture of what it is to be a Catholic, or to live as a Catholic'.[12] The image presented makes Catholicism unattractive and certainly not worthy of intelligent investigation. Also bad, rejecting experiences in church institutions and unsympathetic ministry from critical or pharisaical Catholics are remembered for years by those who experience them. The church with an ugly face does nothing for pre-evangelisation. People are attracted by good people and most are much more likely to become motivated by hope and interested in God through good experiences than through intellectual conviction. Certainly, for a small minority, intellectual conviction might come first, but for most it comes later. My sense is that the emphasis in pre-evangelisation should not be on conversion as on maintaining the dynamism of Christian values and witnessing to Christian convictions in the broader community.

Secondly, what is evangelisation? The early Christians called it *kerygma* or 'proclamation'. The word is derived from *kerux*, which means a town crier, an auctioneer, or a herald. Substantially this is the direct preaching of the faith with the aim of drawing people to Christ and directing them toward conversion. This was a strong emphasis in the New Testament and was inspired by Jesus who told his apostles to 'Go therefore and make disciples of all nations, baptising them' (Matthew 28:19). It is also what Peter was doing in his various sermons in the Acts of the Apostles.[13] However, Peter was preaching in the temple to religious Jews who didn't need pre-evangelisation. They already knew about the time foretold by the prophets and the expected messiah. What was new, and for most utterly scandalous, was that Peter claimed that the man Jesus whom they had crucified was the messiah and had risen from the dead and now sat at the right hand of God.

Nowadays no religious knowledge whatsoever can be presumed and there is a widespread suspicion in Australia about those who are out to make converts. Actually, Catholics are usually sensible about conversion and advise people to think carefully before making a commitment to the church. Bob Dixon estimates that there were about 4790 adolescent and adult converts per year to Catholicism in Australia between 1993 and 2002.[14] This average has probably been sustained or even increased since then. This is where the Rite of Christian Initiation of Adults (RCIA) program has been a Godsend. It takes prospective converts through a structured process that lasts 10 to 12 months and gives them a chance to make a mature and considered decision. The RCIA should not be confused with the Neo-Catechumenate, a quasi-sect operative in a number of Australian parishes. Their aim is to reduce the already-baptised to the status of catechumens and to 'reform' them in an elongated and essentially fundamentalist formation aimed at drawing people into an in-group.

The third step in faith-formation is what was called in early church Greek *didache*, which means 'teaching' or 'doctrine' or catechetical formation in committed faith. This is an important stage in young adult and adult development in which the emphasis is placed on teaching and developing a knowledge of faith. The increasing number of adults and especially women studying theology at a tertiary level indicates that at least among some Catholics there is great interest in developing a deepening understanding of faith. Saint Anselm, archbishop of Canterbury from 1093 to 1109, describes this process as *fides quaerens intellectum*, faith seeking understanding, faith rooting itself in intelligence. This is a strong and deep tradition within Catholicism and it provides the basis for theology. Catholics have never been fideists, that is the notion that religious knowledge depends entirely on blind faith. In genuine Catholicism, faith and reason work together to support belief.

The task of formation in the church's faith involves a complex process. The word 'Catholic' gives us the clue: it is derived from the Greek *katholikos* meaning universal, of the whole. In that sense Catholicism stands as the very opposite of sectarian, particularist and narrow. It is truly itself when it is embracing and inclusive. It involves a commitment to God in Christ and to a way of life that places a person in a community of belief without geographic boundaries, and with a sense of continuity and common history and tradition reaching back through 2000 years to Jesus and the New Testament. It involves a consciousness of God, a sense of the presence of the transcendent in life, a living culture and spirituality, an experience of and feeling for prayer and worship, the sense of a consistent creed expressed through varying theologies and an evolving doctrinal tradition. Catholicism is never static; it is always developing and changing. The greatest of all English theologians, Cardinal John Henry Newman, argues in his 1845 *Essay on the Development of Christian Doctrine* that the more the church grows, develops and changes, the more it becomes truly itself. The *Essay* was published just before his own conversion to Rome. Newman creates an image of doctrinal development through the metaphor of a river. 'It is indeed sometimes said that the stream is clearest near the spring. Whatever use may fairly be made of this image, it does not apply to the history of a philosophy or belief, which on the contrary is more equable, and purer, and stronger, when its bed has become deep, and broad ... here below to live is to change, and to be perfect is to have changed often.'[15] Thus, genuine Catholicism is dynamic, constantly responding to its circumstances, open to the world, the very antithesis of sectarian. What catechesis aims to activate is this sense of Catholicity. This is much more than just knowing doctrine or the myopia of a narrow orthodoxy. It is essentially an ability to place oneself not only in a historical tradition, but also within a community of faith that supports, nurtures and liberates a person for the hope-filled pilgrimage of belief.

We turn now to the world in which contemporary Catholicism lives its faith. There is a sense in which church leaders are right: the modern cultural milieu is difficult and can be very corrosive of faith.

Firstly, referring back to the research already outlined on Gen Y: what emerges is that society is increasingly an accumulation of disparate individuals held together by little more than mutual tolerance, custom, law, regulation and policy in which small, ad hoc, constantly shifting groups of individuals are drawn into co-operation by temporary common interests rather than permanent, mediating communities like the churches. As religious sociologist Michael Mason says:

> Its turned out that society can function with these [minimal] measures in place and can almost dispense with … serious values about the common good. That's regrettable and I think it leads to a rather thin sense of identity in individuals. I'm concerned for Generation Y because they're the first group to grow up in this much more secular, dream-free environment.[16]

Their identity is fragile because it depends on friends and family and not on stable community structures.

The result: individualism is widespread, which in turn leads to insecurity. Insecure people quickly become obsessed with their own well-being, self-fulfilment and immediate family, but detach from the broader community. Their 'hip-pocket' voting pattern reflects this and they seem to have no concept of the common good. Researcher Andrew Singleton says that you see this 'not just in the emergence of suburbs with large houses with kids ensconced with X-boxes and not venturing out to participate, not even playing with their peers in the street, but also in the churches that seem to be popular with young people which emphasise the doctrine that God is desperately interested in things like your financial security, personal well-being, the state of your business affairs and so forth.' Although, as he points out, these same churches do have a strong 'in-group' element built in to their structures.[17]

So how should Catholicism respond to this? The easiest way is to take a stick to it and say that people are inordinately self-obsessed, deeply immersed in a 'culture of complaint', as writer Robert Hughes calls it, and dominated by fear and insecurity. A better response would be to help people re-engage with the values of community. It was precisely this that attracted people to Hadfield parish. People treasured the fact that they were accepted and welcomed and that there were structures in place to maintain the community and provide support when necessary. This doesn't mean that they live in each other's pockets, but it does mean that there is an awareness of a group of people who have a lot in common and who look out for each other. Parishes, schools and all the church's ministries need a strong emphasis on drawing people into welcoming networks, which are there to support them when they really require it, in their crises and life-transitions.

Being a mediating community means more than just accepting and supporting people. It means working together to build up what is good and worthwhile in the wider community and being prepared to confront precisely those factors which underpin and motivate modern individualism, such as neo-rationalist economic theory. As one of the few consistent critics of greed-driven market economics, Catholicism has an important continuing role to play in contemporary society. Its social justice tradition and increasing commitment to ecological issues must be strengthened, developed and applied specifically to local conditions. Catholics believe strongly in the corporate nature of society, in the fact that we are all in this together and have a responsibility for and to each other, that we are not merely atomised individuals caught up in an individualistic struggle against our neighbours.

Modern individualistic society is the product not only of our psychological insecurities and greed, but also of the pervasive influence of post-modernism on education and cultural institutions. Post-modernism is essentially a loose, incoherent agglomeration of ideas that are generally lumped together as a movement. All that is possible are temporary, subjective visions that characterise particular groups and individuals and their specific experiences. This has led to the abandonment of traditional norms of taste and to the breaking down of the division between 'high' and 'popular' culture; nothing is sacred any longer and the distinction between the holy and the profane is considered meaningless. Truth is no longer absolute, but circumscribed, largely by the community in which we live. Put another way metaphysical questions are pointless and meaningless because 'they presuppose that philosophy can be practised independently from history and that an examination of our present way of proceeding might give us an understanding of the 'structure' of all possible ways of proceeding'. Truth, according to post-modernism, is merely the product of a more-or-less unconscious 'intersubjective linguistic consensus' between us all and 'not an accurate representation of something that transcends the human sphere'.[18] It is a deeply secular philosophy and living in such a culture provides a tough ascetical context for anyone trying to live a spiritual life. Faith is relegated completely to the private sphere and spirituality is viewed as faddish, if not completely mad. Post-modernism's impact on truth, art, taste, culture, philosophy, faith and the sacred has been toxic. It has marginalised the so-called 'meta-narratives' (the grand stories and theories which explain the deepest mysteries) and the old absolutes of both science and theology. The dominating paradigm is individual experience. The consequence is that most people prefer personal stories to grand theories which transcend the human sphere, and take us into a kind of absolute, normative world which is supposedly appropriate to all people, times and places.

However, there is a positive side. Modern philosophy highlights the absolute centrality of history. This is in contrast to the past when people understood themselves in the light of static, abstract models, core beliefs and absolute moral norms. Now we see ourselves as involved in an historical process of change. Doctrine is not rigid. This is not necessarily antithetical to Catholicism. The church's tradition is dynamic and changing. As Newman said 'here below to live is to change, and to be perfect is to have changed often'.

The Italian philosopher Gianni Vattimo argues that the sheer relativity of history makes grand narratives and metaphysics impossible and the claim to 'absolute truth' in theology and morality untenable. This, he claims, frees up Catholicism to undergo a *kenosis*, a self-emptying, an abandonment of power and influence which, he says, reflects 'God's renunciation of his own sovereign transcendence' in the incarnation. Thus we are able to hear the word of Christ as a 'historical message of salvation' stripped of its later metaphysical and theological baggage. Vattimo says the early Christians 'believed, as we say in Italian, *sulla parola*, that is "they took [Jesus] at his word"'.[19] What Vattimo succeeds in doing is reminding Catholicism that its theology is rooted in the story of God's intervention in history through Jesus rather than in the pagan philosophical tradition of Plato and Aristotle. It is Jesus who is normative for Christianity, not theories derived from Greek philosophy. Nevertheless, it should be remembered that you can only say this *after* you have understood the contribution that Greek and medieval philosophy have made to the development of Catholicism. The problem is that people tend to rush in and reject this part of the tradition without knowing or understanding the contribution it has made.

What are the implications of this for ministry in Australia? Firstly it means that Jesus and the Scriptures, particularly the New Testament, must be the focus of the church's teaching, proclamation and evangelisation. This is already happening in many Catholic schools and parishes. It is, of course, more difficult in other areas of ministry where you are dealing with vulnerable people, like the sick or the homeless. Here it is the witness of those ministering that is most important. Do they reflect the compassion, sensitivity and goodness of Christ? This brings us back to the issue that as well as caring professionalism, it is Jesus' healing ministry that should be reflected in all that is done in Catholic hospitals, aged-care facilities and charities.

Vattimo's warning about the centrality of Jesus is reminiscent of a theological debate in the 1960s centring on Leslie Dewart's book, *The Future of Belief.*[20] Dewart, like Newman, showed that Christian belief goes through a continuous process of change, sometimes slow, sometimes rapid, but that it is always related to, and only makes sense of itself, in a specific historical context. He shows that after it disconnected itself from Judaism, Christianity found its expression in the Hellenised, neo-Platonist philosophy of the late-Roman world and that it made sense of itself in words and concepts first evolved by classical Greek thought. This evolved further in the Middle Ages. However, these imported intellectual foundations eventually became as important and normative as the person of Jesus himself, and the faith expressed in the Scriptures. In other words, the theological formulae came to be as critical as the personal, transcendent and mysterious reality that they attempted to represent in human words.

An example of the rejection of Hellenism is the way some people criticise the Nicene Creed, the statement of belief that is recited at Sunday Mass that comes from the First Council of Nicaea (AD325). It's hard to find out exactly what upsets them, but I think it has something to do with the way in which they feel forced to use pre-scientific terminology, formulae and distinctions that mean nothing to them. Phrases like 'Eternally begotten of the Father', 'Begotten, not made; of one being with the Father', or 'We believe in the Holy Spirit … who proceeds from the Father and the Son' are simply meaningless to most people today. Our language and discourse today are deeply impregnated with scientific and psychological presuppositions rather than Hellenistic notions of a descending and ascending Christology, the kind of thing summarised in the phrase 'He came down from heaven'. This type of theological discourse makes less and less sense in terms of contemporary science and cosmology. Part of the reason for the success of the writing of Australian theologian, Michael Morwood, is that he has begun the difficult process of re-imaging God and God's relationship with Christ, the Holy Spirit and humankind in ways that make more sense within the context of modern thought and cosmology.[21] Morwood shows how people increasingly find it hard to relate to images of a God in heaven who watches over us, distant and separate, an all-powerful being whose arbitrary decisions are incomprehensible. This image is the product of a circumscribed, closed universe. But contemporary science and astronomy has enlarged our understanding of a continually expanding universe, which contains billions of stars in billions of galaxies which makes it hard to think of a God beyond the cosmos. Another who has explored these ideas is the Irish theologian, Diarmuid O'Murchu.[22]

But many claim that once you abandon traditional formulae you descend into theological chaos. Pope Benedict XVI has talked a lot about the 'dictatorship of relativism'. In his sermon at the Mass for the election of a pope, drawing on the text of the Letter to the Ephesians 'We must no longer be children, tossed to and fro and blown about by every wind of doctrine, by people's trickery, by their craftiness in deceitful scheming' (4:14), the then-Cardinal Ratzinger told his fellow cardinals and the world:

This description is very relevant today! How many winds of doctrine have we known in recent decades, how many ideological currents, how many ways of thinking? ... Every day new sects are created and what Saint Paul says about human trickery comes true! Having a clear faith based on the creed of the church, is often labeled today as fundamentalism. Whereas relativism, which is letting oneself be tossed and 'swept along by every wind of teaching' looks like the only attitude that is acceptable to today's standards. We are moving toward a dictatorship of relativism which does not recognise anything as certain and which has as its highest goal one's own ego and one's own desires.[23]

Benedict, like Vattimo, tends to confuse metaphysical relativism with post-modernism, especially in the reference to egotism and selfishness. He is, of course, very much the classical theologian who lacks a historical and, one suspects, pastoral sense. However, he is right in the sense that relativism is the issue we are facing today. But it is a question of how you interpret it. For Pope Ratzinger the word 'relativism' is a stick, whereas, like Vattimo, I think it might be a harbinger of a process very close to biblical revelation. For the incarnation means that God came to embrace the human condition at a specific time and in a concrete place; in other words God entered within the historical process. Throughout its own history Catholicism has tried to discern what the incarnation means in particular cultural contexts in which the church finds itself. Thus history is essential to the communication of Christian belief and theology, not a mere sideline to be corrected when it contradicts some philosophical or ideological theory. The question is whether embracing the relativity of human history is compatible with Christian faith. I think it is. Christian belief is not focused on particular formulae from past historical periods and cultures, but on the transcendent realities that these words are trying to express. Our culture has long moved beyond Hellenistic concepts such as omnipotence, eternity, immutability and the supernatural, and distinctions between person and nature, essence and existence, substance and accidents. Rhetoric like this is difficult for people like ourselves who think in relational, psychological, evolutionary, historical and functional terms.

So what are we to make of all this? What is its relevance to the future of Catholicism?

First, I think we are dealing with a shift of emphasis here rather than the actual abolition of Hellenistic metaphysics. As a historian I value what the late-Roman and medieval worlds achieved and bequeathed to us. But our culture is much more concerned with experience and process than with metaphysics. As the American theologian Catherine LaCugna says:

> Prior to the shift in philosophical horizon that occurred in the seventeenth and eighteenth centuries Enlightenment, it was assumed that if one could make a metaphysical statement about something – what it is as such or what it is in itself – one had made the truest, most 'real' kind of determination. Today, history, in the sense of 'what really happened', is regarded as the criterion of the most real. Moderns assume that if one cannot determine the historicity of a person, event, or idea, one cannot determine the truth of the matter.[24]

What I want to emphasise here is that a shift of emphasis does not imply the 'abandonment' or jettisoning of something. It simply means that we have already integrated the past, it is already part of that river of which Newman speaks. But the stream has moved onward. Today history and human experience are the norms we use to understand our human predicament and metaphysics is relegated to the background. Essentially our challenge is to formulate a contemporary theology and catechesis that recognises the role of memory and experience. History is about the ever-changing, always complex and often serendipitous interplay of events, processes, circumstances and personalities in extraordinarily diverse and variegated sets of cultural and political contexts. As such it is a much needed antidote and balance to the absolutes of metaphysics.

There is another element at work here. Essentially metaphysical absolutism is about protecting hierarchy. It is about arranging reality in a structured, top-down way which ultimately powerful churchmen interpret. It is essentially about *sacra potestas*: holy power. As Vattimo says 'Metaphysics has survived because … the ancient structure of "power" has survived. So, for instance, the Christian church, being the head of the Roman Empire, could not abandon this structure of power and was not able to develop all the anti-metaphysical implications of Christianity'.[25] But the problem we face is: having transcended Hellenism where do we go from there? If the previous formulae have ceased being meaningful for us, then what are the foundations on which we will base morality and belief? Beyond the fact that many have abandoned the old intellectual superstructures, there are few clues as to what we use to replace the old basis of belief. Dewart and Vattimo are perfectly vague with no really useful suggestions. The solution offered by some is to re-emphasise old absolutes. For instance Cardinal Pell addressing the National Press Club in 2005 said:

> Put very crudely, but with basic accuracy, there is a conviction even among some Church-going Catholics that the Second Vatican Council taught that they can now choose to identify conscience with their personal opinions, and disagree with Church teaching, especially on matters of sexuality and life … The crisis is more publicly apparent in other Christian denominations, eg, in the tragic divisions in the Anglican Churches over the ordination of homosexually active bishops; but the root causes are similar. A fundamental division between liberal and traditional Christians is where to draw the line between immutable tradition or Revelation and what can be changed and updated according to modern understandings. In moral matters this often involves two contrasting views of conscience: the Christian concept, where conscience seeks to discover and do what God commands and a secular view of conscience as personal autonomy, each person's right to define right and wrong for himself.[26]

These caricatures of so-called 'traditional' and 'liberal' stances are not helpful. The church's beliefs are not set in stone, the tradition is a dynamic reality that grows and changes and Pell's notion that somehow there is an immutable reality above history or that revelation is not an ongoing, developing reality is simply not true to Catholic theology.

I think there are other possibilities. The very word 'relativism' is not necessarily pejorative, but suggestive: a relative is someone close, a family member, a person who is an equal and is connected by blood or familial ties. The word 'relativism' is derived from the late Latin *relativus*, an adjective connoting relationship. Relative suggests intimacy and a family community. It conjures up a reminder of that wonderful word for the church in the first centuries: *communio*. Here it is worth noting that it is history that will help us: by searching in the early tradition of the church, especially during the first four centuries, that we may well recover the very approach we need to replace the dominance of Hellenism. We know that the church began as a community of apostles and disciples, men and women who knew each other and were related through their commitment to Christ. As the early church developed, a profound sense of communion and a sharing based on incorporation into the flesh and personhood of Christ evolved in the community. While it is true that a monarchical episcopate emerged early in church history, there was also a profound sense of the diversity of gifts and thus an equality among all the members of the Christian community called together to live the life of God. This is what the early church called *communio*: communion.

The theological basis of communion in early Christianity was essentially Trinitarian. Just as the inner life of God is a subtle minuet of equal persons in a relationship of giving and receiving life, so the Christian community is called to mirror that divine reality here on earth. A number of recent theologians have restored to prominence the Trinitarian basis for the communion of the church, especially Karl Rahner and most recently Catherine LaCugna.[27] Both Rahner and LaCugna argue that the trinity has been marginalised in Christian theology because the doctrine had been divorced from its roots in the economy of salvation, in other words God's plan for the deliverance and fulfilment of all reality. LaCugna argues that from the 4th to the 6th centuries the focus of theology shifted more and more to defining the essence of the trinity, and tended to reflect the absolute, unmoved, impassable God of the philosophers and the metaphysicians, rather than the God of the bible 'who initiated relationship with a people, was open to prayer, petition, and lament, suffered on account of the suffering of the people, became enfleshed in Christ and as Spirit is working to bring about the reign of God'.[28] What we need to recover is a Trinitarian theology of communion, communion within the Godhead and communion with the people of God.

Interestingly, there are resonances here of cosmologist Thomas Berry when he discusses the profound genetic relationships that exist between all living things as the genes that pass on the ever-increasing complexity of life:

> Our bonding with the larger dimensions of the universe comes about primarily through our genetic coding ... It provides ... our capacity for transforming food into energy; in our thought, imagination and emotional life. Our genetic coding enables us to experience joy and sorrow ... It provides the ability to think, speak and create. It establishes the context of our relationship with the divine.[29]

As the quotation from Cardinal Pell above shows, the thing that most troubles those wedded to Hellenism is the fact that the non-absolutist approach seems to relativise so-called 'moral absolutes', particularly those concerned with gender, sexuality and reproduction. While there is some truth to this, it is not necessarily completely so. There is a real sense in which morality is not revealed but is the consequence of the biblical and doctrinal foundations of faith. Jesus hardly ever mentioned specific moral issues except, in passing, those to do with marriage and adultery. The most radical aspect of his teaching going beyond even the commandment of love is his insistence on forgiveness, even of enemies. In contrast to Christianity, the other monotheistic religions, Judaism and Islam, believe in 'an eye for an eye, a tooth for a tooth'. There are many non-violent Jews and Muslims who are committed to peace, but Jesus is the first person in history to say that the vendetta and the desire for revenge are totally inappropriate responses for his followers. As the Jewish literary critic George Steiner says in his wonderful intellectual autobiography *Errata* the most scandalous thing about Christianity is that it believes in forgiveness, even of an enemy. 'Christ's ordinance of total love, of self-offering to the assailant, is, in any strict sense, an enormity. The victim is to love his butcher. A monstrous proposition. But one shedding fathomless light. How are mortal men and women to fulfill it?'[30] Here is the real core of Jesus' moral teaching. Everything else is secondary.

Nevertheless forgiveness can seem like weakness, especially within an extreme terrorist context where the *lex talionis* is seen as justified and even exalted by some Muslims as an aspect of *jihad*. This confronts the Christian with the question of how we should respond to outrages like the 9/11 terrorist attacks on New York, and the Bali, Madrid and London bombings. Should we turn the other cheek? What would that achieve? Personally, I think it would achieve a lot more than the so-called 'war on terror'. Only a truly superior statesperson would have shamed and isolated the terrorists by saying 'I forgive you'. This would have had to have been accompanied by intelligent and astute diplomatic and political work to isolate the terrorists and by appealing to the vast majority of sensible, civilised and peaceful Muslims. Sadly we are not governed by such intelligent political leaders.

To conclude, I want to go back to two points raised at the start of the book. Catholicism has a vast ministerial structure in Australia, and, with the exception of parishes, much of it is supported by government funding in one form or another. Church and state in Australia have achieved a remarkable level of co-operation to provide education, health, aged care and social services. And these are, from the church's perspective, ministries. In the New Testament the word 'ministry' is closely related to the word 'liturgy'. 'To serve others is a "liturgy" laid on the citizens of the Kingdom of God.'[31] Obviously, the word also refers to the worship of the church. So serving one another and worshiping God are intimately related. The clue is in the Greek. The actual word 'ministry' is derived from the Latin *ministerium* which in turn translates the Greek *leitourgia* (from which our word 'liturgy' comes). *Leitourgia* originally meant undertaking a voluntary service as a patriotic duty, which eventually evolved into a compulsory duty. Even in the ancient world the state had a tendency to take over voluntary services.

This is important. The subtle danger that Australian Catholicism faces is that because the government pays for its ministries, its priorities will eventually and inevitably determine the theological priorities of the church. The adage that he who pays the piper calls the tune is particularly apposite here. It probably won't even be the government's intention and it may not result from malice or ill-will, but it is very easy for agendas to be subverted. For the church ministry is a generous service directed particularly towards those who are most in need. Motivated by Christ, everything Catholicism does must be directed towards building up the community and the kingdom of God and liberating people to reach human and spiritual fulfilment. For the democratic state, the priorities are political and are concerned as much with re-election as with service. Also the underlying philosophies are different. Both Labor and the Coalition have moved increasingly to the right and governments of both persuasions are still dominated by economic rationalism and the market, and not by the ideals of community and care for the vulnerable that motivate Christian ministry.

For example, many lower-income Catholics have to send their children to state schools; this fosters a growing belief that Catholic schools have become middle class enclaves where the poor have no place. While governments talk about 'choice' and the church talks about social justice, the fees that parents have to pay simply exclude those families that are struggling to make ends meet. Something similar is happening in private health and hospital care. Again the church is caught between government policy and its responsibilities to care for the poor. The church must maintain its prophetic and critical stance toward society, culture and the ideas that dominate in the marketplace. Organisations like the Saint Vincent de Paul Society have come to the realisation over the last decade and a half that as well as meeting the needs of the most vulnerable, they also have an obligation to confront the structures that create poverty in the first place. This can involve them in conflict with governments that don't take too kindly to public criticism of their policies. Yet this is the task of the church. In many ways Australian Catholicism has developed the ability to be able to hold all of this together. Australian governments, both state and federal, have also contributed much by their good will and their willingness to respect the role of the church. We have never taken the separation of church and state to the absurd lengths to which it has been taken in the United States. For that we can be thankful.

Finally, I want to pick up something I said in the Introduction: Catholicism has remarkable staying power, an ability to survive unmatched by any contemporary institution. If you've been around for just on 2000 years you will have learned a few tricks. There is, of course, a theological explanation for this: that Christ predicted that through his Holy Spirit he would be with the church 'always to the end of the age' (Matthew 28:20). This doesn't mean that the church will be perfect or that parts of it won't wither and die, or that it won't make mistakes. Essentially it means that the Holy Spirit would sustain the church through all the vicissitudes of history in the sense that ultimately the church would not betray Christ or lose the sense of his message completely. It is a case of the Spirit of God assisting the church to make sense eventually out of its own human confusion. Australian Catholics need to keep these theological principles in mind because there is a danger that the magnitude of the task facing the church might engender a sense of pessimism and hopelessness. Catholicism has survived precisely because ultimately it is adaptable and able to change. Often this energy for change comes late in the piece when everything seems to be in dire straits and it may well emerge from the most unexpected source. As Saint Paul says 'God chose what is foolish in the world to shame the wise; God chose what is weak in the world to shame the strong; God chose what is low and despised in the world … to reduce to nothing things that are' (I Corinthians 1:27–28). The other thing in our favour is that the Australian church is just the right size. Not too small so that it becomes incestuous or destroys itself in in-fighting, not too large so that it becomes impossible to change.

Personally, I am optimistic that Catholicism in Australia will survive, certainly with lesser numbers, but with more commitment and ministerial energy. But to achieve that Catholics will require genuine local leadership and a willingness to confront both the difficulties and opportunities that the church faces. My feeling is that we are uniquely placed in Australia to be able to do precisely that.

Notes

INTRODUCTION

1   New South Wales, Legislative Assembly, Hansard, 14 November 2006, p 113.
2   New South Wales, Legislative Council, Hansard, 15 November 2006, pp 3992–94.
3   Richard Rymarz, 'The Impact of World Youth Day: A Twelve Month Follow-up of Under 18 Australian WYD 2005 Participants', *Australasian Catholic Record*, 84/4, October 2007. See also 'Who Goes to World Youth Day? Some Data on Under-18 Australian Participants', *Journal of Beliefs and Values*, 28/1, pp 33–43.
4   Jo Grainger on *Encounter*, 'The Pilgrim Way – World Youth Day 2005', ABC Radio National, 18 September 2005.
5   See Paul Collins, *Upon This Rock. The Popes and their Changing Role*, Melbourne: Melbourne University Press, 2000, pp 122–23.
6   Geoffrey Robinson, *Confronting Power and Sex in the Catholic Church. Reclaiming the Spirit of Jesus*, Melbourne: John Garratt Publishing, 2007, pp 235–36.
7   Paul Collins, *No Set Agenda*, Melbourne: David Lovell, 1991, p 4.

1 CATHOLICISM IN ACTION

1   Saint Vincent de Paul <http://www.vinnies.org.au>.
2   Saint Vincent de Paul <http://www.vinnies.org.au>, go to Matthew Talbot Homeless Services. See also 'Changing Face of Homelessness' in *Online Catholics*, 13 December 2006 for the statistical breakdown.
3   Based on the Society's figures on its website <http://www.vinnies.org.au>.
4   Ernie Smith, *Miracles do Happen: A Priest Called Smith*, North Blackburn: Collins Dove, 1993.
5   Sue Williams, *Mean Streets. Kind Heart: The Father Chris Riley Story*, Sydney: HarperCollins, 2003, and *World Beyond Tears. The On-Going Story of Father Chris Riley*, Sydney: HarperCollins, 2005.
6   David Horton (ed), *The Encyclopedia of Aboriginal Australia*, Canberra: Aboriginal Studies Press, 1994, Vol 2, p 995. See also Edmund Campion, 'A Father to the Poor and Dispossessed', obituary for Father Ted Kennedy, *Sydney Morning Herald*, 19 May 2005.
7   John Bede Polding to Rosendo Salvado, 1863. Quoted in Frances O'Donoghue, *The Bishop of Botany Bay. The Life of John Bede Polding, Australia's First Catholic Archbishop*, Sydney: Angus and Robertson, 1982, p 170.
8   Quoted in Patrick O'Farrell, *The Catholic Church and Community. An Australian History*, Sydney: UNSW Press, 1992 revised edition, p 120.
9   Edmund Campion, *Australian Catholics. The Contribution of Catholics to Australian*

Society, Melbourne: Viking, pp 96–104.

10 For Francis Xavier Gsell see *Australian Dictionary of Biography*, Melbourne: Melbourne University Press, Vol 9, pp 135–36. See Gsell's autobiography, *The Bishop With 150 Wives*, Sydney: Angus and Robertson, 1956.

11 Author interview with Father John Leary, MSC, 30 April 2007.

12 For evidence of Father Mervyn Bailey's language work see Australian Institute of Aboriginal and Torres Strait Islander Studies Library, MS 848.

13 Ernest Ailred Worms, *Australian Aboriginal Religions*, translated from the German by MJ Wilson, D O'Donovan, M Charlesworth, Kensington, NSW: Nelen Yubu Missiological Unit, 1986.

14 Quoted in *Australian Aboriginal Religions*, p xvi.

15 See *Encyclopaedia of Aboriginal Australia*, Vol 1, p 218 (for Coniston) and p 387 (for Forest River). For a detailed examination of the Coniston massacre see John Cribbin, *The Killing Times*, London: Fontana, 1984.

16 Quoted in Barry Hill, *Broken Song. TGH Strehlow and Aboriginal Possession*, Sydney: Vintage, 2003, p 737.

17 The 2001 figures are taken from Robert E Dixon, *The Catholic Community in Australia*, Melbourne: Christian Research Association/Openbook Publishers, 2005, p 65. The 2006 figure is my estimate based on 23 per cent of Aborigines being Catholic.

18 Archdiocese of Sydney, *A Quiet Place. Australian Retreat Directory*, Revised 2001. See <http://www.cathcomm.org/cathcomm/retreats>.

19 John Garvey, 'Of Monks and Madmen', *Commonweal*, 18 May 2007.

20 Information from Catholic Health Australia <http://www.cha.org.au/site> and from consultation with its staff. The actual statistics change often in this area and numbers may not be exact at the time of publication.

21 Lyn Allison, 'The Socratic Forum', 15 November 2006. See <http://www.democrats.org.au/speeches>.

22 Francis Sullivan, 'Unfair Criticism Overlooks Catholic Church's Proud History', *The Australian*, 20 January 2007. See also the 'Attack on Hospitals Ill-informed', *Catholic Leader*, 21 January 2007.

23 Caritas Australia Financial Report for the year ended June 2006.

24 Church statistics based on the 2007–08 *Official Directory of the Catholic Church in Australia* (Catholic Directory).

25 Figures from the archdiocesan homepage <http://www.melbourne.catholic.org.au>. See also the Catholic Directory, 2007–08, pp 273–342 and p 718.

26 Figures from 2001 census, Saint Thomas More Parish Profile, July 2005. I visited Hadfield on 30 March 2007 and met with parish staff. Much of the information comes from that discussion.

27 Dixon, *Catholic Community*, p 112.

28 Quoted in *Letters for Lent. Women and Men Transformed in Christ*, Melbourne: Archbishop's Office for Evangelisation, 2007, pp 20–21.

29 Author interview with Bill Brady, MSC, 29 March 2007.

30 Doug Conlan, 'Sunday Mass Round on the Rabbit-Proof Fence', *Eremos Magazine*, No 78, February 2002.

31 Most of these statistics are drawn from the National Catholic Education Commission (NCEC) 2006 Annual Report, pp 20–24. They reflect the situation in 2005.

32 NCEC, 'Catholic Schools Enrolment Trends, 2003'.

33 Statistics from Australian Bureau of Statistics (ABS), 2006.

34 I visited MacKillop Catholic College on 28 May 2007 and information comes from author interviews with Rita Daniels (principal), Michelle Marks (campus head, Wanniassa), Paul Goonan and Mark Pickham (Religious Education co-ordinators).

35   DF Bourke, *A History of the Catholic Church in Victoria*, Melbourne: Catholic Bishops of Victoria, 1988, p 322.
36   Catholic Directory, 2007–08, p 719.

2 CATHOLICS IN AUSTRALIAN SOCIETY

1   The Pope's remarks were first published in Italian in the Vatican newspaper, *L'Osservatore Romano*, 27 July 2005. An English version appeared later on the Vatican website <http://www.vatican.va>.
2   Mark Latham, *The Latham Diaries*, Melbourne: Melbourne University Publishing, 2005, p 114.
3   Gary Bouma, *Australian Soul. Religion and Spirituality in the Twenty-first Century*, Melbourne: Cambridge University Press, 2006, pp 46–47.
4   Gary Bouma and Beverley R Dixon, *The Religious Factor in Australian Life*, Melbourne: MARC Australia, 1986, p 166.
5   David Millikan, *The Sunburnt Soul. Christianity in Search of an Australian Identity*, Homebush West: Anzea Publishers, 1981, pp 9–10.
6   ABS, 'Census Shows Non-Christian Religions Continue to Grow at a Faster Rate', Media Fact Sheet, 27 June 2007.
7   Bouma, *Australian Soul*, p 66.
8   ABS, Media Fact Sheet, 27 June 2007.
9   Bouma, *Australian Soul*, p 67.
10   Bouma on *The Religion Report*, ABC Radio National, 4 July 2007.
11   See Ian Markham, 'Shades of Grey: The Pope, Christian Ethics and the Ambiguity of Human Situations', Trinity Papers Number 8, Trinity College, University of Melbourne, 1997, p 5.
12   Markham, 'Shades of Grey', p 17.
13   Enid Lyons, *So We Take Comfort*, London: Heinemann, 1965, p 235.
14   O'Farrell, *Catholic Church and Community*, pp 208–09.
15   Neville Hicks, *'This Sin and Scandal'. Australia's Population Debate 1891–1911*, Canberra: Australian National University Press, 1978, p 157; ABS, *Family Formation: Trends in Fertility*, 24 June 1996; Anne O'Brien, *God's Willing Workers: Women and Religion in Australia*, Sydney: UNSW Press, 2005, p 37.
16   John T Noonan, *Contraception. A History of Its Treatment by the Catholic Theologians and Canonists*, Cambridge, Mass: Harvard University Press, 1965, p 406.
17   *Royal Commission of Inquiry on the Decline of the Birth Rate and on the Mortality of Infants in New South Wales*, Sydney: Government Printer, 1904, 2 volumes.
18   Hicks, *Sin and Scandal*, p 157.
19   O'Brien, *God's Willing Workers*, p 37. See Chapter 2.
20   Hans Mol, *Religion in Australia. A Sociological Investigation*, Melbourne: Thomas Nelson, 1971, pp 249–50.
21   O'Farrell, *Catholic Church and Community*, p 377.
22   John Warhurst, 'Catholic Voices in Australian Politics', McCosker Oration, National Conference of Catholic Social Services Australia, 16 October 2006.
23   Haydon Manning, '"Aspirational Voters" and the 2004 Federal Election', *Australian Review*, 4 July 2005.
24   John Warhurst, 'Religion in 21st Century Australian National Politics', Australian Senate Occasional Lecture Series, 5 May 2006, pp 5–6.
25   Brian Toohey, 'Politicians Focus on our Sinful Ways', *Sydney Morning Herald*, 6 June 2004.
26   Marion Maddox, *Sunday*, Nine Network, 3 July 2005.

27 There is some confusion as to their exact number because of category confusion in the 2001 census. The ABS Media Fact Sheet of 27 June 2007 gives their numbers at 1 per cent in 1996.

28 ABS, Media Fact Sheet, 27 June 2007.

29 Kevin Rudd, 'Faith in Politics', *The Monthly*, October 2006.

30 Kevin Rudd, 'Howard's Brutopia', *The Monthly*, November 2006.

31 Clive Hamilton, 'Churches Could Hold the Key to Salvation for the Left', *Eureka Street*, 31 October 2006.

32 Warhurst, McCosker Oration, 16 October 2006.

33 See John L Allen's comments, 'Day Five: Benedict's Critique of Capitalism no Surprise', *National Catholic Reporter*, 13 May 2007.

34 Bill Uren, *Compass*, ABC TV, 10 December 2006. For Joe Hockey's speech see Australia, House of Representatives, Hansard, 6 December 2006, pp 55–57, and for Michael Hatton's see Australia, House of Representatives, Hansard, 6 December 2006, pp 64–69.

35 Australia, House of Representatives, Hansard, 6 December 2006, pp 117–19.

36 Australia, House of Representatives, Hansard, 6 December 2006, pp 119–20.

37 Australia, Senate, Hansard, 30 November 2006, p 16.

38 Quoted on the *7.30 Report*, ABC TV, 23 April 2007.

39 Amanda Lohrey, Quarterly Essay 22, *Voting for Jesus. Christians and Politics in Australia*, p 63.

40 Response to *Voting for Jesus*, Paul Collins in Quarterly Essay 23, pp 83–87.

41 Allison, 'The Socratic Forum'.

42 Peter Carnley, *The Structure of Resurrection Belief*, Oxford: Clarendon Press, 1987.

43 See John L Allen, 'The Real Ratzinger Revealed', *The Tablet*, 16 April 2007.

44 Australian Catholic Bishops' Conference (ACBC), *Go Tell Everyone. A Pastoral Letter on the Church and the Media*, 2006, p 2.

45 Barney Zwartz, *The Age Blogs*, 'The Religious Write. Reporting with Integrity', 22 July 2007. See <http://blogs.theage.com.au/thereligiouswrite>.

46 Barney Zwartz profile, *The Age Blogs*. See <http://blogs.theage.com.au/thereligiouswrite>.

47 Geraldine Doogue, 'Unfinished Business – The Church in Public Life', <http://www.catalyst-for-renewal.com.au/geraldine_doogue.htm>.

48 Michael Gilchrist, *Lost! Australia's Catholics Today*, Melbourne: Freedom Publishing, 2006, p 10.

3 CATHOLICS ADRIFT

1 The phrase comes from Peter Steinfels, *A People Adrift. The Crisis of the Roman Catholic Church in America*, New York: Simon and Schuster, 2003.

2 ACBC (Marie McDonald editor), *Woman and Man. One in Christ Jesus,* Sydney: HarperCollins, 1999.

3 All quotations in this paragraph taken from the Executive Summary of *Woman and Man*, pp vii–ix.

4 ACBC, *Woman and Man*, p 187.

5 ACBC, *Woman and Man*, pp 175–76.

6 Reported in *The Tablet*, 28 July 2007, p 29.

7 Benedict XVI, Talk at General Audience, 14 February 2007.

8 Benedict XVI, TV interview, 13 August 2006. See Deutsche Welle <http://www.dw.world.de>.

9 ACBC, *Woman and Man*, p 178.

10 Ordination of Catholic Women (OCW), 'Duty Bound to Lead. Towards a Renewed

Ordained Ministry', Canberra: OCW, 2006, p 2.

11 Robert Dixon, Sharon Bond, Kath Engebretson, Richard Rymarz, Bryan Cussen, Katherine Wright, *Research Project on Catholics Who Have Stopped Attending Mass*: Melbourne, ACBC Pastoral Projects Office, 2007, pp 26–28.

12 ABS, 'Marriages', *Australia 2005*.

13 Statistics from Relationships Australia, *The Rest. Relationship Statistics*, Vol 63, November 2006.

14 Congregation for the Doctrine of the Faith (CDF), 'Letter to Bishops Concerning Reception of Holy Communion by Divorced and Remarried Members of the Faithful', 14 September 1994, para 4.

15 Catholic News Service, 'Divorced Catholics Must be Welcomed in Parishes, Pope tells Priests', 27 July 2005.

16 Mark A Sargent, 'Vengeance Time. When Abuse Victims Squander Their Moral Authority', *Commonweal*, 20 April 2007.

17 John Doherty and Julian Wellspring, 'Canonical Reflections on the Experience of Priests with Towards Healing & Encompass', *The Swag*, Autumn 2007, pp 34–38. A reply from the Professional Standards Committee by Bishop William Morris was published in *The Swag*, Winter 2007.

18 Australian Catholic Bishops' Conference (ACBC) and Australian Conference of Leaders of Religious Institutes (ACLRI), 'Towards Healing. Principles and Procedures in Responding to Complaints of Abuse Against Personnel of the Catholic Church of Australia', National Committee for Professional Standards, December 2000.

19 See *The Tablet*, 15 September 2007, p 37.

20 Frank Brennan, SJ, *Acting on Conscience. How Can we Responsibly Mix Law, Religion and Politics?* Brisbane: University of Queensland Press, 2007.

21 Sandro Magister, 'Benedict XVI's First Visit to Latin America', *Chiesa*, 20 April 2007 <http://chiesa.espresso.repubblica.it>.

22 See Eric Hodgens, 'Seminary Facts, Factors and Futures'. See also 'An Alternative to the Priest', *Online Catholics*, Issue 28, 1 December 2004 and 'The Bishops' Last Chance', Issue 112, 12 July 2006.

23 Edward Schillebeeckx, *Ministry. Leadership in the Community of Jesus Christ*, New York: Crossroad, 1981, p 37.

24 For a discussion of this issue see Richard A Schoenherr, *Goodbye Father. The Celibate Male Priesthood and the Future of the Catholic Church*, New York: Oxford University Press, 2002.

25 Jane Anderson, *Priests in Love. Roman Catholic Clergy and Their Intimate Friendships*, New York: Continuum, 2005, pp 36–37.

26 Anderson, *Priests in Love*, pp 48–49.

27 Conversation with Father Williams, 28 August 2007. The generic term 'Latin Mass' covers both the pre-Vatican II so-called 'Tridentine Mass' and the renewed liturgy celebrated in Latin. The term 'Tridentine' here refers to the Council of Trent (1545–63).

28 Quoted in Alain Woodrow, 'No Sign of Rapprochement', *The Tablet*, 28 July 2007, p 14.

29 Rita Ferrone, 'A Step Backward. The Latin Mass is Back', *Commonweal*, 17 August 2007.

30 Gilchrist, *Lost!*, pp 180–81.

31 Eric Hodgens, 'An Alternative to the Priest', *Online Catholics*, 28, 1 December 2004.

32 These figures are based on charts in Bourke's *History of the Catholic Church in Victoria*, p 228.

33 Bourke, *History of the Catholic Church in Victoria*, p 297. Almost all diocesan priests

work in parishes. Priests who are members of religious orders on the other hand often have specialist training and work in a wide variety of ministries including parishes.

34 *Official Year Book of the Catholic Church of Australasia, 1961–62*, Sydney: EJ Dwyer, 1961.

35 United States Conference of Catholic Bishops (USCCB), Press Release, 6 June 2000. Figures from the Georgetown University-based Center for Applied Research in the Apostolate (CARA).

36 Catholic Directory, 2007–08, p 718. Here it should be noted the summary figures in the Catholic Directory, 2006–07 (p 650) are inaccurate due to inconsistent reporting.

37 This is based on an estimate that about 1820 priests from both dioceses and religious orders are engaged full-time in parish ministry.

38 Catholic Directory, 2007–08, p 718. I can only find 30 diocesan priests listed in the archdiocesan section of the Directory (pp 217–35) with 17 in parishes and 13 retired or on leave.

39 'A Parish with no Priest', *Compass,* ABC TV, 5 March 2006.

40 The figures for Wilcannia–Forbes and Townsville are based on the diocesan webpages.

41 William Morris, Advent Pastoral Letter, 2006.

42 *Pastor Bonus* (paragraph 79), which deals with the functions of the various Vatican departments.

43 Information on the Chaput visit came from personal contacts within the Toowoomba diocese. I have verified the information using alternative sources.

44 *Official Year Book of the Catholic Church of Australasia, 1961–62*, archdiocese of Canberra–Goulburn statistics.

45 Dean R Hoge and Aniedi Okure, *International Priests in America. Challenges and Opportunities*, Collegeville: Liturgical Press, 2006.

46 Jane Anderson, 'Which Priests for Our Church?', *Compass: A Review of Topical Theology*, 37 (2003), pp 24–28; 'Our Father Who Art from Overseas', *Online Catholics*, Issue 134, 12 December 2006. The Bishops' National Commission for Clergy Life and Ministry issued a paper on 17 October 2005 by Father Peter Brock, 'Some Issues to Consider When Welcoming Priests Coming from Overseas'.

47 Hoge and Okure, *International Priests*, p 123.

48 Dean R Hoge, *Experience of Priests Ordained Five to Nine Years*, Washington, DC: National Catholic Educational Association, 2006. Mary L Gautier and Mary E Bendyna, 'The Class of 2007: Survey of Ordinands to the Priesthood', a report for the USCCB. CARA, March 2007.

49 Porteous quoted in Gilchrist, *Lost!*, pp 177–78.

50 Paul Stanosz, 'Lets be Candid About the Candidates', *Commonweal*, 1 December 2006.

51 Dean Hoge, *Initiative Report*, 4 March 2007. The book referred to in the article is *The First Five Years of the Priesthood. A Study of Newly Ordained Catholic Priests*, Collegeville: Liturgical Press, 2002.

52 Andrew Greeley, 'Young Fogeys. Young Reactionaries, Aging Radicals – the US Catholic Church's Unusual Clerical Divide', *Atlantic Monthly*, January/February 2004.

53 Donald B Cozzens, *The Changing Face of the Priesthood*, Collegeville: Liturgical Press, 2000, pp 97–110.

54 Cozzens, *Changing Face*, p 105. John Boswell, *Christianity, Social Tolerance and Homosexuality*, Chicago: University of Chicago Press, 1981.

55 'Teach the Faith and Christian Morality in this Age "of Worrying Disorientation", says Pope', in *Asia News* 12 May 2007. See <http://www.asianews.it>.

56 Statistics from John Allen, 'All Things Catholic', *National Catholic Reporter*, 11 May 2007.
57 *God's New Man. The Election of Benedict XVI and the Legacy of John Paul II*, Melbourne: Melbourne University Publishing, 2005, pp 35–53. For the Greeley quotation see p 47.

4 WHY DO CATHOLICS LEAVE THE CHURCH?

1   Paul Collins, *William Bernard Ullathorne and the Foundation of Australian Catholicism*, PhD thesis, Australian National University, 1989, p 143.
2   Mol, *Religion in Australia*, p 11. O'Farrell's figures (*Catholic Church and Community*, pp 59, 184, 280) are lower and reflect New South Wales.
3   Mol, *Religion in Australia*, p 14.
4   Dixon, *Catholic Community*, pp 97–98.
5   O'Farrell, *Catholic Church and Community*, p 208.
6   O'Farrell, *Catholic Church and Community*, p 203.
7   For Moran see *Australian Dictionary of Biography*, Vol 10, pp 577–81. See also the recently published biography by Philip Ayres, *Prince of the Church. Patrick Francis Moran*, Melbourne: Miegunyah Press, 2007.
8   See *Acta et Decreta Concilii Plenarii Australasiae, habiti apud Sydney AD 1885*, Sydney: F Cunninghame, 1887.
9   *Acta et Decreta*, paragraph 240.
10 *Acta et Decreta*, paragraphs 13 and 238.
11 *Acta et Decreta*, paragraph 141.
12 *Acta et Decreta*, paragraphs 144, 145 and 148.
13 O'Farrell, *Catholic Church and Community*, p 205.
14 Dixon et al, *Stopped Attending Mass*, pp 14–15.
15 Dixon et al, *Stopped Attending Mass*, p 3.
16 Statistics from Dixon, *Catholic Community*, pp 96–98.
17 Dixon et al, *Stopped Attending Mass*, p 4. See also Dixon, *Catholic Community*, p 91.
18 Dixon et al, *Stopped Attending Mass*, pp 18–20.
19 Dixon et al, *Stopped Attending Mass*, pp 22–27.
20 Dixon et al, *Stopped Attending Mass*, pp 29–31.
21 Collins, *God's New Man*, p 48. See pp 35–53.
22 Dixon et al, *Stopped Attending Mass*, pp 29–35.
23 Dixon et al, *Stopped Attending Mass*, pp 37–42.
24 Dixon et al, *Stopped Attending Mass*, pp 65–66.
25 Dixon et al, *Stopped Attending Mass*, p 50.
26 Dixon et al, *Stopped Attending Mass*, p 66.
27 See Collins, *Between the Rock and a Hard Place. Being Catholic Today*, Sydney: ABC Books, 2004, p 78. See pp 78–85.
28 Quoted in Collins, *Between the Rock*, p 80.
29 Andrew Greeley, *The Catholic Imagination*, Berkeley: University of California Press, 2000.
30 Michael Mason, Ruth Webber and Andrew Singleton, *The Spirit of Generation Y: Young People's Spirituality in a Changing Australia*, Melbourne: John Garratt Publishing, 2007.
31 Mason et al, *The Spirit of Generation Y*, p 12 and pp 15–17.
32 Mason et al, *The Spirit of Generation Y*, p 39.
33 Mason et al, *The Spirit of Generation Y*, pp 68–70.
34 Michael Mason, *The Spirit of Things*, ABC Radio National, 13 August 2006.

35   Mason et al, *The Spirit of Generation Y*, pp 73–75.
36   Mason et al, *The Spirit of Generation Y*, p 76.
37   Mason et al, *The Spirit of Generation Y*, pp 80–82.
38   Mason et al, *The Spirit of Generation Y*, pp 129–31.
39   Mason et al, *The Spirit of Generation Y*, p 134.
40   Mason et al, *The Spirit of Generation Y*, p 136.
41   This material is drawn from a Christian Research Association press release (12 April 2007). Unfortunately I found out too late about *Putting Life Together: Findings of Australian Youth Spirituality Research*, Nunawading, Vic: Christian Research Association, 2007 to discuss the book in detail.
42   Lisa Bryant, 'Survey Finds Growing Spirituality in European Youth', *VOA News*, 27 July 2002.
43   *Religion News Blog* <http://www.ReligionNewsBlog.com> 9 August 2002.
44   Andrew Greeley, 'Catholic Youth Celebrate Faith', *Chicago Sun-Times*, *Daily Southtown*, 28 July 2002.
45   Dean R Hoge, 'How Laity See the State of American Catholicism', *Initiative Report*, 3 March 2007, at <http://www.nplc.org/commonground/pdf/InitiativeReport-Mar 2007.pdf>. The book referred to is William D'Antonio, James Davidson, Dean Hoge, Mary Gautier, *American Catholics Today: New Realities of Their Faith and Their Church*, Lanham, MD: Rowman and Littlefield, 2007.
46   Dean Hoge on *The Religion Report*, ABC Radio National, 18 October 2006.
47   Mason, *The Spirit of Things*.
48   Andrew Greeley, 'New Hope for Catholic Schools', *Chicago Sun-Times*, *Daily Southtown*, 2 March 2007.
49   William J Lines, *Patriots. Defending Australia's Natural Heritage*, Brisbane: University of Queensland Press, 2006.

5 HOW SHOULD THE CHURCH RESPOND?

1   John L Allen, *All Things Catholic*, 'Struggle to Reassert Traditional Catholic Identity Scores two Wins', 13 July 2007. See *National Catholic Reporter* <http://www.ncrcafe.org>.
2   George Pell, 'Conscience: The Aboriginal Vicar of Christ', 2004 Fisher Lecture, Fisher Society, University of Cambridge.
3   William Barclay, *New Testament Words*, London: SCM Press, 1964, p 174. For *koinonia* see pp 173–76.
4   Gilchrist, *Lost!*, pp 14–15.
5   Gilchrist, *Lost!*, p 133.
6   Gilchrist, *Lost!*, p 11.
7   David Jaeger quoted in Allen 'Catholic Common Ground Lecture'. See also Gilchrist, *Lost!*, p 11.
8   Daniel Finn quoted in John L Allen's 'Theologians Challenged to Set the Pace for Inclusive Conversations', *All Things Catholic*, 21 June 2007.
9   Sandro Magister, 'Ratzinger's Revolution Passes with Flying Colors', 20 October 2005; Sandro Magister, 'Dearest Pastors and all the Faithful of the Catholic Church in China …', 30 June 2007, *Chiesa Online* <http://chiesa.espresso.repubblica.it>.
10   Collins, *God's New Man*, pp 35–53.
11   See Collins, *Between the Rock*, pp 8–10 for the story of the Synod.
12   For leadership see Collins, *Mixed Blessings*, Melbourne: Penguin Books, 1986, pp 72–74, *No Set Agenda*, Melbourne: David Lovell, 1991, pp 34–38 and *Papal Power*, Melbourne: HarperCollins, 1997, pp 139–43 and pp 149–51.

13   Collins, *No Set Agenda*, p 35.
14   Benedict XVI, 'Homily of His Holiness Benedict XVI', Vatican Basilica, 7 May 2006. See <http://www.vatican.va>.
15   Statistics from Our Sunday Visitor's *Catholic Almanac* 2007, p 333.
16   National Council of Priests (NCP) Australia, 'Reflections on the Lineamenta', January 2005.
17   'Split in Push for Married Priests', *Sydney Morning Herald*, 27 January 2005.
18   Statistics from John L Allen, 'Lay Ecclesial Ministry and the Feminization of the Church', *All Things Catholic*, 29 June 2007. Allen doesn't make clear whether these statistics include teachers in Catholic schools.
19   John N Collins, *Diakonia: Reinterpreting the Ancient Sources*, New York: Oxford University Press, 1990 and *Are All Christians Ministers?*, Sydney: EJ Dwyer and David Lovell, 1992. Although I have known John for many years, he is not a relation.
20   Collins, *Are All Christians Ministers?*, p 1.
21   Schillebeeckx, *Ministry*, pp 72–73.
22   Here I am following the interpretation of Dr Graham English in his 'Catholic Religious Education in Australia', 4 June 2007. See <http://www.catholica.com.au>.
23   Anne O'Brien, *Blazing a Trail. Catholic Education in Victoria 1963–1980*, Melbourne: David Lovell, p 13.
24   O'Brien, *Blazing a Trail*, p 14.
25   See John N Cullinane, *Goulburn School 'Strike', The Inside Story*, Canberra: Archdiocese of Canberra and Goulburn, Catholic Education Office, 1989.
26   O'Brien, *Blazing a Trail*, p 109.
27   Campion, *Australian Catholics*, p 235.
28   Campion, *Australian Catholics*, pp 235–36.
29   English, 'Catholic Religious Education in Australia', 4 June 2007. See <http://www. catholica.com.au>.
30   Marcellin Flynn, *The Culture of Catholic Schools: A Study of Catholic Schools, 1972–1993*, Sydney: Saint Pauls Publications, 1993, and Marcellin Flynn and Magdalena Mok, *Catholic Schools 2000: A Longitudinal Study of Year 12 Students in Catholic Schools, 1972–1982 – 1990–1998*, Sydney: Catholic Education Commission, 2002.
31   Flynn and Mok, *Catholic Schools 2000*, pp 239–41.
32   Flynn and Mok, *Catholic Schools 2000*, pp 245–47, 250–51.
33   Flynn and Mok, *Catholic Schools 2000*, p 248.
34   Flynn and Mok, *Catholic Schools 2000*, pp 251–53.
35   Flynn and Mok, *Catholic Schools 2000*, pp 281–83.
36   Flynn and Mok, *Catholic Schools 2000*, pp 286–87.
37   Flynn and Mok, *Catholic Schools 2000*, p 308.
38   English, 'Catholic Religious Education in Australia'.
39   Flynn and Mok, *Catholic Schools 2000*, pp 315–16 and 308–09.
40   MacKillop Catholic College, *Senior School Handbook*, 2008, p 10.
41   Niola Curtis, 'Teaching RE – What does it Mean Today?', The Australian Association for Research in Education <http://www.aare.edu.au/00pap/cur00138.htm>.
42   *Catholic Schools at a Crossroads*, pp 5, 8, 6.
43   *Catholic Schools at a Crossroads*, p 8.

6 DOES AUSTRALIAN CATHOLICISM HAVE A FUTURE?

1   See Daniel Donovan, 'What is the Nature of the Crisis Facing the Church?', *Catholica Australia*, 29 July 2007. See <http://www.catholica.com.au>.
2   Robinson, *Confronting Power and Sex in the Catholic Church*.

3   Eric Hodgens, 'The Bishops' Last Chance', *Online Catholics*, Issue 112, 7 July 2006.

4   The exception to this was that from the 17th century the Congregation De Propaganda Fide (the Roman department supervising mission countries) appointed bishops in mission territories or countries where Catholics were a persecuted minority, eg, Britain.

5   Collins, *Papal Power*, pp 174–75.

6   Morris West, 'One Man's Voice', *Eureka Street*, August 1994.

7   Benedict XVI, Apostolic Letter *Summorum Pontificum*, translation in *USCCB NewsLetter*, May/June 2007, p 18.

8   Here I have used the Jerusalem Bible translation rather than the New Revised Standard Version.

9   Julian of Norwich, *Showings*, edited and translated by Edmund Colledge and James Walsh, New York: Paulist Press, 1978, p 229.

10   John Paul II, *Ecclesia in Oceania*, paragraphs 8 and 13 quoted in *Catholic Schools at a Crossroads*, pp 11–12.

11   See Alfonso M Nebreda, *Kerygma in Crisis*, Chicago: Loyola University Press, 1965.

12   'Peregrinus', *Catholica Australia*, 15 August 2007. See <http://www.catholica.com.au>. It was actually Brian Coyne, editor of *Catholica Australia* who first drew my attention to what a dreadful image of Catholicism many of these webpages present.

13   The English scholar CH Dodd popularised the use of the term *kerygma*. See his *The Apostolic Preaching and Its Developments. Three Lectures with an Eschatology and History*, London: Hodder and Stoughton, 1936.

14   Dixon, *Catholic Community*, p 112.

15   John Henry Newman, *An Essay on the Development of Christian Doctrine*, London: Longmans, Green, 1909 edition, p 40.

16   Mason, *The Spirit of Things*.

17   Andrew Singleton, *The Spirit of Things*, ABC Radio National, 13 August 2006.

18   Santiago Zabala (Editor), *The Future of Religion*, New York: Columbia University Press, 2005, p 4.

19   Gianni Vattimo in Zabala, *The Future of Religion*, pp 52, 53.

20   Leslie Dewart, *The Future of Belief. Theism in a World Come of Age*, London: Burns&Oates, 1967. In 1967 Gregory Baum edited *The Future of Belief Debate*, New York: Herder&Herder.

21   Michael Morwood's latest book is *From Sand to Solid Ground: Questions of Faith for Modern Catholics*, Melbourne: Spectrum, 2007.

22   Diarmuid O'Murchu, *Quantum Theology*, New York: Crossroad, 1996. Revised 2004.

23   Ratzinger quoted in Collins, *God's New Man*, pp 127–28.

24   Catherine Mowry LaCugna, *God For Us. The Trinity and Christian Life*, San Francisco: HarperCollins, 1991, p 4.

25   Vattimo in Zabala, *The Future of Religion*, p 62.

26   George Pell, National Press Club, Canberra, 21 September 2005.

27   Karl Rahner, *The Trinity*, London: Burns&Oates, English translation, 1970.

28   Catherine Mowry LaCugna, 'The Practical Trinity', *The Christian Century*, 15–22 July 1992, p 681.

29   Thomas Berry, *The Dream of the Earth*, San Francisco: Sierra Club Books, 1988, p 196. See Collins, *God's Earth. Religion as if Matter Really Mattered*, Melbourne: HarperCollins, 1995, pp 158–59.

30   George Steiner, *Errata. An Examined Life*, London: Phoenix, 1998, p 59.

31   Barclay, *New Testament Words*, p 178.

All websites were accessed on 3 October 2007.

Index